Treasures
In
Words

Poems, Prayers,
and Personal Stories

Teresa E Lavergne

ISBN: 978-0-9966237-5-9
ISBN-13: 978-0-9966237-5-9

I would like to dedicate this book to some people who have inspired me and ministered so much to me:

To my sisters, Frankie Otis and Ramona Kellogg, who have braved many storms in life and have come out of them victorious through their faith in Christ.

To Carol Schwartz, a friend to whom we are extremely indebted for all her creative endeavors in the Lord's service, alongside us in ministry. She is a great blessing to all who know her.

To my dear friend April Broussard, who assisted us in children's ministry for many years. She continues to shine brightly as a light for Jesus, especially to children.

To Sherry Dugan, who has cheered me on and encouraged me so many times, through her faith in the Lord and His goodness. She and her husband Jeff have been such a help to us, in many ways.

To Cathy Simmons, who was my Good Samaritan. She picked me up and carried me by her prayers, when my heart was broken and I was bleeding internally from grief. Many times, the Lord spoke through her to me in the very words I used in my prayers the night before!

To Guy--- my husband, best friend, counsellor, constant companion, and partner in ministry. You have loved me well and I am so grateful. You have loved me even at my worst. I appreciate who you are in Christ more than ever.

I am blessed to know all of you.

Other books by Teresa Lavergne:

The Angel in the Garden

The Antique Mirror and the Ancient Secret

In the Garden of His Grace

Other books by Guy and Teresa Lavergne:

Act Upon a Story: 60 Bible Skits for Ministry

Act Upon a Story: A Series of Skits about Joseph

Act Upon a Story: A Collection of Christmas Plays

ACKNOWLEDGMENTS

All Scripture quotations, unless otherwise indicated, are taken from the Holy Bible, New International Version®, NIV®. Copyright ©1973, 1978, 1984, 2011 by Biblica, Inc.™ Used by permission of Zondervan. All rights reserved worldwide. www.zondervan.com The "NIV" and "New International Version" are trademarks registered in the United States Patent and Trademark Office by Biblica, Inc.™

Scripture taken from the New King James Version®. Copyright © 1982 by Thomas Nelson. Used by permission. All rights reserved.

Scripture taken from the New Century Version®. Copyright © 2005 by Thomas Nelson. Used by permission. All rights reserved.

Scripture quotations marked (GNT) are from the Good News Translation in Today's English Version- Second Edition Copyright © 1992 by American Bible Society. Used by Permission.

"Scripture quotations taken from the New American Standard Bible® (NASB),
Copyright © 1960, 1962, 1963, 1968, 1971, 1972, 1973, 1975, 1977, 1995 by The Lockman Foundation
Used by permission. www.Lockman.org"

Scripture quotations marked (NLT) are taken from the Holy Bible, New Living Translation, copyright ©1996, 2004, 2015 by Tyndale House Foundation. Used by permission of Tyndale House Publishers, Inc., Carol Stream, Illinois 60188. All rights reserved

IN HIS MIND

Carefully and skillfully the life-long craft began;

Needlepoint by needlepoint, together all threads ran.

But still it often puzzled me

How all the threads would meet;

For all I saw were dangled ends---

A jumbled mass, unneat.

Then one day I caught a glimpse

Of the Master's whole design;

And I marveled at its well-made plan.

My life was in His mind.

"Your eyes saw my unformed body;
all the days ordained for me were written in your book
before one of them came to be."

Psalm 139:16

GRACE

I disobeyed the laws of the king of this land.

It was only right that I should die.

I trembled

When I learned what I had done.

There was no escape from justice,

No hiding place from him,

Whose law is pure, whose word is truth,

He will not wink at evil.

There was nothing left for me

But surrender.

I fell down low before him

When they brought me to his throne.

I lay down like a dog at his feet.

But he took my hand and raised me

He led me to his banquet,

And seating me beside him,

He turned to me and said,

You shall not be my servant

But my friend.

A PURE HEART

Lord, make our lives a revelation of Your character.

Give us Your passions and Your desires.

Recreate our hearts---fashion them like Yours.

Reorder our thinking---make it like Yours.

Clothe us with Your glory and radiance.

Prepare our hearts to worship in spirit and in truth.

We give you our whole heart.....with no divisions.

Wash us with the "water of the Word." Confirm the authority of Your word so that people will trust You more and more.

Let us sense Your splendor, and your ever-present help to lead and guide us.

Help us come into a greater awareness of Your power in motion. It is not stagnant---it is working constantly on our behalf.

Give us a pure heart----for the pure in heart are the ones who can see God---the ones who can discern what He is doing.

"Blessed are the pure in heart,
for they will see God."

Matthew 5:8

SPARROWS

How can he know

When a sparrow falls---

Or the hairs of my head?

How do you stand

Before a God like that.

All my arguments against him

Melt away

When I see him hold a sparrow

In His hand.

"Two sparrows cost only a penny, but not even one of them
can die without your Father's knowing it."

Matthew 10:29 NCV

ALIVE

It was the time of the Great Depression, and they were a farming family. Everyone worked hard in order to survive. At Christmas, their prize was an apple or an orange. Their clothes were often made from the material of feed sacks. A doctor's services could not be afforded, so one of their children died. They had no running water and did not even have the luxury of an outhouse. For adventurous games, the children were chased by bees and killed snakes. This was my father's childhood.

He was one of the few children who were able to attend college, and his major was petroleum engineering. When WWII began, he enlisted in the Navy to avoid being drafted into the army. After his naval ship was disabled from enemy fire, he didn't see any more of the war. I am glad for that, because what he saw on his ship was horrifying enough. After the war, he went to work for an oil company, and there he met my mother who was the switchboard operator.

I asked him once why he married her, and he said it was because she was nice to him. Those few words speak volumes.

My father's ambition as a young man was to have a house with a bathroom in it! He certainly succeeded in that. In the early sixties, we had a new brick house with all the modern features typical at that time. But it wasn't enough; my parents began a spiritual journey and visited different brands of churches. At last, they found what they were looking for: they found Christ----not a religion, but a Person. It was the testimony of the janitor at a church, who convinced them of the reality of Jesus, and the joy He gives.

Our social life as a family now became intertwined with this church and its activities. A few years later, we were on the way to my grandmother's house, and came to a dangerous curve in the highway, and the unthinkable happened. Another car came into our lane, and we could not avoid it. It was a head-on collision at 70 miles per hour.

I came out of a three day coma to discover that I had no mother anymore. She died a few hours after the wreck from internal injuries. I was so numb that I couldn't even cry. I don't think I cried until our first child was born. When I held that little baby and felt so much love for her, it made me miss having someone who loved me that much. I went without it for so long, and had to learn to survive without it, that I had forgotten how it felt.

Though I knew my parents' faith was real, it wasn't until I was a depressed and desperate teenager that I surrendered my life to Christ. I am so thankful that He pursued me until I gave in! He never let me go. He gave me a husband who loves Jesus, and a calling to children's ministry, all at the same time. I was a college art student at the time, but He changed my aspirations and direction. (He hasn't yet revealed all His plans for this later time period in our lives, but I believe He is a father who likes to surprise His children with good things!)

I didn't tell our daughter about her grandmother's death until I thought she was old enough. I knew there would be hard questions to answer. She wanted to know why God would allow such a thing; wasn't He strong enough to prevent evil from happening? If He was, why didn't He stop it? Does He truly protect His children? These are tough theological questions. Some of them, I can't answer yet. I won't know the answer until I enter Eternity, where all truth will be known.

I could only point to the truth I do know; that our world is corrupted by evil because our ancestors chose independence from God's Word instead of obedience. The problem of evil started with us, not with God. But He is the one who is still reaching out to rescue us from our bad choices of independence from Him. He sacrificed what He loved most---His only Son---in order to rescue us.

Jesus' disciples certainly did not understand at the time why God let His Son die. When we don't understand, we have to trust that He is good, and that the end result will be good. My daughter knew the story of Joseph, so his life gave a clear example to show this. Bible stories are a foundation for faith, so make sure your children know them!

But I still had an underlying, irrational feeling---some kind of primitive notion that made me secretly uneasy about my mother's early death---as if we inherit our parents' destinies. She died at age 39; and somehow in my subconscious mind, I felt predestined to an early death.

The Lord proved otherwise.

We were on a short vacation to the beach in Florida when it happened; we were caught in the middle of a high-speed chase on the highway. I was reading a book, and Guy was driving. I looked up in shock as our yellow and brown station wagon flew into the ditch---along with several other cars. There were cars in the grassy median that dipped below the highway on the left, as well. On the opposite side, in the highway going the other way, I saw the backs of about half a dozen police on motorcycles, speeding by as they vanished down the road.

Guy was so shaken, he could hardly speak. It had happened so fast. The lady whose car was just behind us in the ditch spoke up first. She told us she was afraid she was going to hit us when she had to get off the road so quickly. There was little space between our cars. In an instant, six cars had to get off the road simultaneously.

In a little while, a deputy pulled up behind us all to check and make sure that we were all okay, and we found out what happened. There was a car coming straight at us at 100 or more mph; he was on the wrong side of the highway. The police who were riding on motorcycles caught up with him, and shot his tires out to stop him.

We were so relieved that this vacation did not end in a death trap for us, or for these other people traveling alongside us. When I later reflected on this near death experience, the Lord spoke through this verse to me:

"I shall not die, but live,
And declare the works of the Lord."
Psalm 118:17 NKJV

"I sought the Lord, and he answered me;
he delivered me from all my fears."
Psalm 34:4

JESUS

He signed the contract;

Paid the price---

Now I'm his.

He repossessed me

From destruction,

Cleared the debt I owed;

I give up freely every right and claim

To myself;

I abandon myself to Him!

Without regret---

I surrender with joy.

To be His slave

Is worth more than all my freedom,

To be near Him.

I never want to leave His house again.

I'm completely captivated

Utterly fascinated

Intoxicated

With belonging to this Man.

WE WERE SLAVES

We were all sold into sin slavery, by the decision of our first ancestors, Adam and Eve.

There is only One who has the credentials to pay the ransom for our freedom.

He was the sinless, perfect Sacrifice.

Jesus came from Heaven as a human, and gave His life to rescue us.

In order to belong to Him, we must become His servant.

Yet He loves us not only as a servant, but as a friend.

Not only as a friend, but as His family.

Not only as family, but as His bride---His cherished love.

What a joy it is to belong to Him!

"Jesus replied, "Very truly I tell you, everyone who sins is a slave to sin." John 8:34

EXPANSION

Lord, we love You because You first loved us.

We want to make You smile.

Enlarge our hearts to hold as much as we can contain of You in these meager human vessels.

Help us to love You back and trust in Your all-surpassing goodness. There is truly no one like You.

Your goodness cannot be measured. Nothing could contain it for measurement!

The universe is expanding but Your goodness is still greater.

Let our lives give people a glimpse of it.

"But we have this treasure in jars of clay
to show that this all-surpassing power
is from God and not from us."

2 Corinthians 4:7

INCLUDED

The greatest adventure of my life began when I was seventeen---I met Jesus and I began to live for Him—or should I say live with Him. He came into my life and changed me.

This was just before my senior year of high school.

At some point between that last year of high school, and my second year of college, I had a girls' sleep-over at my house. (I was still living at my father's house at the time.)

We didn't really have a youth group at my church, but I had a few friends from church who I invited to this sleepover. I had seen a new girl at church from another state. She was staying for a while with her married sister, who brought her to our church. I barely knew this girl, or anything about her--- but for some strange reason I had a sudden urge to invite her to the sleepover.

So I invited her, and she came. I don't remember any of the particulars about that night---what we did, or what we ate--- but it must have been a happy time for us all.

The chain of events that occurred from that night still astounds me.

I found out later what happened.

This teen girl was visiting her sister because she had been having some problems, and she was very unhappy. But while she was here, she gave her life to the Lord, and He gave her joy. Her older sister was thrilled to see her so happy.

I was so shocked when I found out that the catalyst for her decision was a simple invitation to a sleep-over. That one act of acceptance---of simply including her---made all the difference in how she felt accepted by the Lord.

I was so grateful to the Lord that He prompted me to invite her. And even more so when I heard what happened shortly after she went back home.

This teen girl had a heart attack and died. I never knew teenagers could die from that, but she did. I know that I will meet her again in Heaven someday, and we will talk about that sleep-over!

I am so grateful that the Lord has included me and you in His plans. His plans are to ensure that people will know how much He wants to include them, too, in His eternal plans.

He doesn't want anyone to be left out of that.

"Instead he is patient with you,
not wanting anyone to perish,
but everyone to come to repentance."

2 Peter 3:9

LIVING TESTIMONIES

He was an enigma, a puzzle to people.

They had to discover his secret inside.

What gave him this joy?

What made him smile?

The answer so simple, it can't be denied.

To some, she was clear---

As transparent as glass.

She made it apparent, no need to ask.

The hope was revealed,

The hope of her heart,

The Light of the world,

When all is dark.

The name she calls on,

The name she loves—

His name is Jesus, God's only Son.

"Salvation is found in no one else, for there is no
other name under heaven given to mankind
by which we must be saved." Acts 4:12

SHEKINAH GLORY

Your beauty is too great for me, oh Lord

There is none beside You.

You make my heart skip

Like a child in the summer;

You make me want to dance before You

In the sanctuary.

You make me want to leap with joy

Like a babe in the womb,

At the prospect of life.

The joy I have in You

Is like a sunburst inside me

Exploding in light and warmth—

I cannot contain it!

It overwhelms me like a river

That has overflown its banks;

It sings inside me

Like a high clear melody

Coming down from the hills.

Show me Your glory, oh Lord!

Shekinah glory in the temple.

How does a person describe what it feels like to encounter the Presence of God? This poem was my attempt to do this.

I think I wrote this just after I had been up in the Ozark Mountains for a college student retreat.

We were under an open-air Tabernacle during a heavy rain and thunder storm.

The camp was nestled in a high valley, with mountains looming all around us.

And afterwards, the clouds were misty and the hot summer air had become cool, the foliage was glistening and shiny green, and the creek was no longer dry, but full and flowing.

The whole earth around us was refreshed.

The cloud of His presence is the Shekinah glory, and He sends the rain to water the earth.

And our hearts are refreshed.

CANA OF GALILEE

I hear the sounds of your market place
The voices of the crowds----
The calling of the merchants, the bleating of the sheep
The shuffling of sandaled feet,
Dusty clouds around them.

I hear the laughter at the wedding
Where He first made the wine--
The sounds of celebration and of people eating---
How He loved these people who were needing
The life He longed to give.

These people so moved him, He could not resist
His involvement in their lives.
He told them of Heaven while they fished or ate;
He welcomed their children no matter how late;
No one was too insignificant.

I hear the sound of His resonant voice,
As He taught them with stories of feasts
And harvests and kingdoms and servants and birds.
They followed Him closely and cherished His words,
Of God and His love for this world.

Cana of Galilee, I envision you
Much more than a small fishing town.
You were a rendezvous---a meeting space;
A reconciliation place--
Between the heart of God and man.

Before I surrendered my life to the Lord, I had never really "seen" who Jesus is.

The Word of God didn't mean much to me.

But after I gave my life to Him, suddenly I could see Him in His Word----for the first time ever!

I couldn't get enough of seeing Him and what He is like.

The Word of God became like a panorama, unfolding in three dimensions before me, extending further and further into infinity.

I pray you will see Jesus too.

"What Jesus did here in Cana of Galilee was the first
of the signs through which he revealed his glory;
and his disciples believed in him."

John 2:11

PRINCE CHARMING

I was always looking for him---
Seeking constantly,
The man with earnest eyes---
The one who'd set me free.

Hunting for that face in crowds,
I watched the people from afar—
Looking for him at nighttime,
Hoping in some star.

To the thirsty in the desert
Mirages are what could have been;
But every time that I drew near,
I saw they were only men.

He had been there all the time.
In my searching, I was blind---
I looked for castles, and men on black steeds---
But one so sincere, I could not find.

They say he's just a carpenter
But I see in him a Prince.
He proved his love to me,
And honored my existence.

No candy or flowers, he proved it with blood.

They condemned him and spit in his face---

No greater love could ever be known;

At this execution, he died in my place.

Yet he lives; the grave is now empty.

Death could not withstand his love.

I wait for him to take me

To his home in Heaven above.

Jesus is the eternal Bridegroom, who is preparing a place for us in His father's house.

"There are many rooms in my Father's house; I would not tell you this if it were not true. I am going there to prepare a place for you." John 14:2 NCV

He will return to escort us there.

"After I go and prepare a place for you, I will come back and take you to be with me so that you may be where I am." John 14:3 NCV

HOLDING ON

The enemy tried to kill me when I was in college.

It was as if he had his agent waiting right there at the intersection of Bertrand and South College, as I was on my way home from a UL Chi Alpha worship and prayer meeting.

The truck never even paused at the stop sign; it just flew out and rammed the side of my old 1965 hand-me-down car. That old car had no power steering; I had built up my arm muscles by driving that car.

The lack of power steering was extremely dangerous in this case; the car went out of control on impact. No other cars were on the road at the time; a miraculous occurrence in itself for South College Road! If there had been any other cars that night, it would have been disastrous.

I didn't have the arm strength to stop this careening car as it fish tailed down the 4 lane road, and it was pulling to the right. I realized I would go off the road if I didn't hold on…. An insidious voice spoke inside my head: "Just let go and die." I knew in that instant who said these words, and I retaliated with a scream at the top of my lungs: "JESUS!!!!!!"

Suddenly it felt as if stronger hands than mine took hold of the wheel and held it steady until I was finally able to stop the vehicle….before I got to the intersection of South College and Congress Street.

Another amazing thing: When the police got there, I was totally calm and cheerful. I was not shaking at all. The poor guy in the truck who ran the stop sign was white with shock.

The impact had smashed in the side of my car, right behind the driver's seat. The entire front left window had shattered, and all of the glass was on the floor behind my seat. It flew over my shoulder without hitting my face. There was not a single injury anywhere.

There are definitely times in our lives when we are meant to let go....and times when we are meant to HOLD ON!

"Yet I am always with you;
you hold me by my right hand."
Psalm 73:23

It is the most assuring thing to realize that Jesus will not let go of us, and no one can snatch us away from Him.

We are safe in His hands, in His care.

"My sheep listen to my voice; I know them, and they follow me. I give them eternal life, and they shall never perish; no one will snatch them out of my hand. My Father, who has given them to me, is greater than all; no one can snatch them out of my Father's hand. I and the Father are one."
John 10:27-30

CLARITY

Lord, please clarify Your will with precision, to our spirits.

Help us to be affected by Your Word, and not the culture of the world.

Help us to have a greater dedication to following You and not fads or trends.

Help us to choose pursuits that bring You delight.

You are deserving of a Bride without blemish! We can't beautify ourselves---please do this by the Holy Spirit's power and through Your love for us.

Heal our seared consciences and make our hearts new---vibrant and alive.

Remove all falsehood and pretension from our hearts.

Strip our hearts of favoritism, criticism, and condescension.

Remove contempt, disdain and scorn for others.

Give us Your power to love and forgive.

Deliver us from a false morality that is religious and not spiritual.

Free us from self-righteousness that masquerades as godliness, causing confusion and robbing us of Your peace and joy.

Help us to seek You to receive Your grace, which is of priceless value.

Let Your magnificent qualities shine through us.

Amen.

Hallelujah!
For our Lord God Almighty reigns.
Let us rejoice and be glad
and give him glory!
For the wedding of the Lamb has come,
and his bride has made herself ready.
Fine linen, bright and clean,
was given her to wear."

Revelation 19:6-8

"Nothing that is impure will enter the city..." Revelation 21:27 GNT One day, we will be made as pure as the Lord is....but we are not that way yet.

Forgiveness must be a part of earthly existence because we still have impurities---we are not perfected yet because Jesus is not finished with us; He is still working on us.

Imperfect people cannot demand perfection from others---we constantly need to forgive, as we are constantly forgiven.

Forgiveness brings healing and restoration; God is a forgiving God and wants us to be that way, too.

Heaven comes down when we forgive.

AGAPE

What is my life?

A walk in the darkness.

A short light---that will be snuffed out---

In time.

I know what I want it to say to the world---

That God can be trusted---and loved.

Help me be a peacemaker, building hope in people---

A triumphant supernatural calm.

When the world comes to a climax

When the coil's wound tight and taut

And there's no more leisure

In people's faces---

Or their ways---

When they finally can see

As in prisoner camps

In the chaos of war---

How their values have been blind---

Let them find in me a resource of strength,

Through the words that You have said.

Help me start preparing now

In the fat and well-fed times, for the lean.

Everything here is temporary; destruction is coming.

But the greatest force that has ever existed

Is in the heart;

Only love will remain.

"Love does not delight in evil but rejoices with the truth. It always protects, always trusts, always hopes, always perseveres. Love never fails." 1 Corinthians 13:6-8

This is agape love; the love of God.

We can't produce it; we can only find it in the person of the Lord, who is always willing to share His love.

His love is our hope.

"And hope does not put us to shame, because God's love has been poured out into our hearts through the Holy Spirit, who has been given to us." Romans 5:5

IMPRESSIONS

When I was a child, sometimes my family went to "camp meeting"---this was a church service in an open-air pavilion we called a tabernacle. These meetings were at night, and I remember the yellow light halos from naked light bulbs, hanging by long wires from the beams overhead. I remember the whirr of many large fans, and how it made me sleepy. But you couldn't really sleep, because there was a sense of excitement, and far too many other sounds of rustling paper fans, very fussy babies, exuberant clapping, and emphatic amens.

There was one man---Brother Teague, we called him---who would get so excited that he would walk around the outer perimeter of the area, waving a white handkerchief and exclaiming "Glory".

Did we think of him as weird or crazy? No; in fact he was one of the people whose faith was considered most genuine. The Lord had touched his life, and he was not ashamed to express his gratitude fervently. He made an impression on me as a child, of being very, very real.

If I remember right, this camp meeting was held at the same place there was a children's camp in the summer. I went to this kids' camp the summer after my mother died. One day at camp, my friend let me wear her pretty new tennis shoes. During some free time, some children were walking across a field to look at a concrete stage out there, and I followed them. They began climbing up and jumping off the stage, so I did too. I jumped off one side and then I screamed----- there was a board nailed to my foot.

I don't remember much after that. I am told that my friend's mother took me to the closest emergency clinic, and that it took several nurses to hold me down so they could give me a tetanus shot.

The main thing I remember is how ashamed I felt that I caused so much trouble for people, due to not having my own mother. It was a very inconvenient thing to not have a mother.

The other thing I remember is that I was very embarrassed that I ruined my friend's shoes. My blood had stained them on the inside, and now they had a big nail hole in the sole.

Jesus always made it clear to adults that He did not think of children as too much trouble or inconvenient. Brother Teague didn't think so either, and we children were attracted to him. He always kept pennies in his pocket, and he would give us a penny for every Scripture verse we would recite to him. He was delighted to hear us say our verse.

I was so excited when I learned all of Psalm 1, and could say it for him. All these years, I have never forgotten that. Brother Teague made me feel as if this was one of the world's greatest accomplishments, because he valued God's Word.

There is so much truth capsulized in this one Psalm:

"Blessed is the man who walks not in the counsel of the ungodly, nor stands in the path of sinners, nor sits in the seat of the scornful;

But his delight is in the law of the LORD, and in His law he meditates day and night.

He shall be like a tree planted by the rivers of water, that brings forth its fruit in its season, whose leaf also shall not wither, and whatever he does shall prosper.

The ungodly are not so, but are like the chaff which the wind drives away.

Therefore the ungodly shall not stand in the judgment, nor sinners in the congregation of the righteous.

For the LORD knows the way of the righteous, but the way of the ungodly shall perish."

Psalm 1 NKJV

Recently, I was thinking about this psalm, and I read some articles about trees. Did you know that trees never stop growing? If they stop, they will die.

And the older they are, the faster they grow. That is encouraging if you think of it in spiritual terms. Our spiritual growth accelerates as we get older, and we will continue producing fruit for God's Kingdom.

I could shout and wave, at that thought!

And I really like how Brother Teague invested in children--- he was planting trees.

"They will be called oaks of righteousness,
a planting of the LORD for the display of his splendor."

Isaiah 61:3

LIFE

I began

Working on my project as a boy.

Careful to nurture and cultivate it,

Rearrange and change it;

I worked hard to better it.

It was my own, my very own,

And no one had the rights to it but me.

Eventually

I achieved through it, and gained through it

A house and job, a wife and kids,

Prestige.

But still I kept on working; I had no time for less.

I brushed aside the inner voice still speaking.

When my wife died, I merely sighed

And kept on working.

There was no end to my obsession.

The children married and moved away

And still I labored on.

At last when I was old and gray

And thought I might retire from this,

The thing I'd never planned on happened---

Someone stole my life.

This poem is loosely based on the parable Jesus told in Luke 12:16-21:

"The ground of a certain rich man yielded an abundant harvest. He thought to himself, 'What shall I do? I have no place to store my crops.'

"Then he said, 'This is what I'll do. I will tear down my barns and build bigger ones, and there I will store my surplus grain. And I'll say to myself, "You have plenty of grain laid up for many years. Take life easy; eat, drink and be merry."'

"But God said to him, 'You fool! This very night your life will be demanded from you. Then who will get what you have prepared for yourself?'"

"This is how it will be with whoever stores up things for themselves but is not rich toward God."

I HEARD HIS VOICE

No, it wasn't an audible voice---but it was so loud inside my head that I woke up from a deep sleep instantly alert and totally awake.

It happened when I was in college, and it is one of those special memories I will always cherish. The Lord made Himself so real to me that night, I can never forget it.

I was sleeping in a bunkbed, on the bottom bunk, when this happened. We were at a retreat for the students who were part of the UL Chi Alpha Christian Fellowship.

The Lord woke me up, and told me to get up on the top bunk and pray for the girl who was sleeping up there, because she was going into an epileptic seizure. So I did, and her restless jerking symptoms went away.

She never woke up, and I quietly went back to my bed and back to sleep.

Later, I have thought about this, and realized how amazing it all was. The Lord didn't need me to stop a seizure; He could have done that without my help! But He included me in His ministry to this girl. We are co-laborers with God.....an incredible privilege. 1 Corinthians 3:9

This also shows us the value of prayer---we are working with the Lord when we pray.

This new girl had begun to visit the Chi Alpha meetings, and so I had invited her to come on the retreat. She had recently gotten disentangled from a very bad situation; she had been living with a guy who was on drugs. She had severe epilepsy; in the past, she had a grand mal seizure and fell, breaking her jaw. If I remember right, her boyfriend did not take care of her at all during this episode, so she moved out of his apartment.

Then she showed up at the meetings, looking for a new life. My friends and I did our best to encourage her in her faith and relationship with the Lord. When we went on the retreat, however, she would not listen to our advice. She wanted to be healed so badly from epilepsy that she refused to take the preventative medicine for seizures.

We certainly didn't condemn her for wanting to be healed, but we strongly urged her to take the medicine. When the Lord healed her, it would be confirmed. Until then, she might be putting herself at risk of a grand mal seizure, and further injury. Not only did she not take the medicine, but she insisted on sleeping on the top bunk!

She was not healed on that retreat. (In fact, she had another seizure on the campgrounds.) And after the retreat, we didn't see much of her any more. When I called to check on her at her mom's apartment, I found out she had gone back to the guy on drugs. Her mother firmly exclaimed, "She is very happy!" And I knew from her tone of voice that she wanted no interference with her daughter's "happiness."

I learned something from this: Sometimes healing is a test of our desires. Some people want the Lord's benefits, but they don't want Him. When they don't get what they want, they desert Him.

I know now that I don't want "happiness"----I want fulfillment. And that can only be found in the person of Jesus.

He IS righteousness, peace, and joy.

He is everything we long for.

And I love His Voice!

"Then I heard the voice of the Lord saying, "Whom shall I send? And who will go for us?"

And I said, "Here am I. Send me!"   Isaiah 6:8

"Listen and hear my voice;
pay attention and hear what I say."

Isaiah 28:23

"Whether you turn to the right or to the left, your ears will hear a voice behind you, saying, "This is the way; walk in it."

Isaiah 30:21

"Then a cloud appeared and covered them, and a voice came from the cloud: "This is my Son, whom I love. Listen to him!" Mark 9:7

OUR FATHER WHO ART IN HEAVEN

We're much too busy for Him—

Too preoccupied to heed Him---

We've got our jobs and occupations

Our children and our homes;

Who wants to bother with Him?

He'd only interrupt our plans and try to run our lives---

No, we want to be the boss.

So we hide ourselves from Him

In our garden of chores and duties;

Mustn't admit to anyone

How naked we are without Him

Or how much we really need Him.

It's just so much easier to make your own god

And bow down and worship yourself;

Or put Him beneath you and say that your sense

Of justice is better than His;

But He has more grace than we credit Him for;

His righteousness so far exceeds us.

We can't understand Him; we don't know His ways.

So we try to ignore Him and pretend He's not there

Yet He still seems to get in our way---

Constantly watching and longing and wooing us---

So that we can be with Him.

"Then the man and his wife heard the sound of the LORD
God as he was walking in the garden in the cool of the day,
and they hid from the LORD God among the trees of the
garden. But the LORD God called to the man,
"Where are you?"

Genesis 3:8-9

I wonder what kind of form the Lord had at this time---his
steps made a sound. They could hear Him walking in the
garden. Was this their special time together with Him? But
now they were afraid and hid from Him. Then they heard His
voice---the Voice of love---calling to them, "Where are you?"

Some of us are still hiding from Him; we don't want to admit
we are wrong. We're afraid of Him, so we don't respond to
Him. We ignore His voice when He is calling out to us.

"Today, if you hear his voice, do not harden your hearts."
Hebrews 4:7

NEW CLOTHES

As a young adult, my shopping skills were severely underdeveloped. Impulsive decisions led to many unsatisfying acquisitions….and an empty wallet.

I had to wear my mistakes----like light-colored pastel pants to a mixed-media art class. When I walked out of that class, I looked like a bib-less child who has been decorated with his dinner!

And I made yet another mistake. I bought a swimsuit that was a little too revealing. It was very cute, no doubt about that, and the next larger size might have eliminated the problem; but you can't return swimsuits. And I had no money to buy another one.

I put myself in a dilemma, because my summer schedule of activities included swimming---and not just with girls. I didn't want to make anyone---or myself---uncomfortable.

So I asked the Lord about it.

That same day, an acquaintance came to my house with a swimsuit. She told me that it didn't fit her anymore, and she thought maybe I would want it. It was very cute.

And guess what? (You probably guessed already) It fit perfectly----and modestly.

The Bible says a lot about clothing---most of it is symbolic.

It's something to investigate.

DESPERATE PRAYER

Lord, You are my Life.

You are my Hope.

You are my Rock.

You are my Destiny.

Hold me in Your arms of comfort and consolation.

Hide me in the shelter of Your presence.

Destroy the enemy's plans to harm me and render me useless.

Display the power of Your Kingdom through awesome deeds of goodness.

Lead me in Your path of mercy and compassion.

Settle any agonizing issues for Your servant's sake and for the sake of Your name.

I am clinging to You.

Lord, hear my cry and answer me...

You will not despise a broken spirit---or the utterly helpless who cry to You.

I look to You.

DIVORCE IS A NORM

Time has mellowed me;

I'm not the rebel that I was.

My contemporaries

Still battle with desires

Of glory and of grandeur

In the culture of the world;

They live to create

To innovate

The newest style of living

The latest mode of thought

And changing with the ideals

Of each successive stage

People split apart like atoms

In a bomb.

I consider that I'll have success

When I've made a family

That can last;

When I've overcome

With what I have

With what I am

Where so many have fallen---

In defeat.

This poem is not intended to condemn anyone who has suffered a divorce. If you have gone through the pain and grief of divorce, my heart goes out to you. This poem is a statement about our culture, which is so conducive to divorce. While I was a full-time student at UL, most of my professors in the art department (that was my major) either were recently divorced, getting divorced, or on the verge of divorce. This made me re-evaluate my idea of success.

It also made me careful about what I looked for in a future husband. Guy definitely met my requirements, and still does. We are grateful for over forty years of being life-partners for God's Kingdom, to love and support each other. I'm thankful the Lord put us together to share the Gospel--- the Good News of His love and mercy.

"He has shown you, O mortal, what is good.
And what does the LORD require of you?
To act justly and to love mercy
and to walk humbly with your God."

Micah 6:8

HOLD ON TO THOSE EGGROLLS!

In my last year of college, I didn't have much money for food. By that time, I was living in an apartment with two other girls who also went to UL. (It was called USL back then)

One time, we were down to only a bag of corn meal, some oil, and some honey. So we ate corn pancakes fried in oil and topped with honey---not a bad solution, after all.

Another time, we only had popcorn until payday. (That was less interesting; I wonder if manna tasted like plain popcorn)

Oh, I could have gone and presented a Dire Need and Charity Case at my dad's house; but I was not about to ruin the Adventure of Being Independent!

Guy came to spend some time with me one evening, and he was broke, too. It must have been all those long distance calls from New Iberia to Lafayette. (That was the Stone Age when we had rotary dial phones and everything between towns was long distance)

So we scraped up $6.00 to buy 6 egg rolls at the Chinese take-out place. We got those egg rolls in a Styrofoam container, (yes, they had those back then) and drove back to my place.

Guy was driving a big old dark blue Hippie van at that time. You had to step up high to get in. Well, as I was getting down from my side, I suddenly had a horrible vision in my mind----and I blurted out, "Don't drop the egg rolls!"

There was complete silence from the other side of the van.

I couldn't see Guy anymore. So I went around the back of the van, and saw my vision had come true: Guy was crawling around on the parking lot by the van---and he was picking up egg rolls.

The egg rolls did what egg rolls do---they rolled---out of the box and under the van.

We were very hungry, and that was all we had----so we dusted them off and we ate them. (And I lived to tell the tale!)

I knew Guy and I were supposed to get married---but there was a brief time when I doubted. (It wasn't the egg roll time!) I sensed the Lord asking me, "Will you love Guy for Me?"

I said yes. I'm not sure how good a job I've done at that----but it has been an adventure loving each other and serving God together---one that I would never trade.

And we have learned to Hold On to Love.

(And to laugh when you drop the egg rolls!)

"Let love and faithfulness never leave you;
bind them around your neck,
write them on the tablet of your heart.
Then you will win favor and a good name
in the sight of God and man."

Proverbs 3:3-4

LIGHTS IN THE RAIN

The lights look very nice

In the rain

Especially the ones

On the old army barracks

We use for classes.

That's something

I never noticed in the sunshine.

They remind me of warm things---

Retreats I have been to,

The meeting of old friends.

There's no one

Out in this rain

It's dusk-grey and my jeans

Are soaked up to the knees.

But the warmth of the lights steadies me

Calms me

Reminds me

Of the Joy that I know.

A JOURNEY

When Guy and I got married, we were practically children---twenty somethings who barely knew how to write a check. We didn't really have a plan of any kind.

I loved my artwork, and I was trying to finish getting an art degree from UL, and Guy was a carpenter who wanted to build houses. We had no idea of how our lives should go.

The only sure thing we knew is that we wanted to work with children, and we loved Jesus. These things were the constant; they were the unchanging principles of our lives.

Even our honeymoon was not really planned. We spent the first night in Baton Rouge in a "luxury" room that wasn't so luxurious, and then Guy asked me where I wanted to go. One summer I had gone to a S.A.L.T. conference in north Arkansas, and I remembered how beautiful it was there. I said, "Let's go to the mountains in Arkansas."

So we did, even though we really didn't have enough money to do that. We scrimped on meals and motels. (We actually found some inexpensive places that were clean)

We traveled up highway 7 in Arkansas---a very narrow winding road through the mountains. You often couldn't see what was just around the bend in the road. Once we stopped at a "scenic view" site along the road, and an elderly man came down the hill and talked to us. He was a Christian, and it was so encouraging to meet him. He suggested that we go to Silver Dollar City and the "Passion

Play". We had not thought of going to Silver Dollar City, but we decided this was timely advice and we headed that way.

Late in the afternoon, we were back on the winding road, and the sun was beginning to go down and the shadows were getting darker. I had a wistful thought; I said to Guy, "Wouldn't it be nice to stay in a mountain cabin?"

We rounded the bend in the road, and there in front of us was a hanging wooden sign swinging in the breeze and it said: "Mountain Cabin." Isn't the Lord funny?

And it was the cutest cabin---very rustic and quaint and authentic. (It even had mountain cabin spiders!) And the owners were Christians, and they prayed with us when we left.

We went to Silver Dollar City and the "Passion Play", and then we headed home. In north Louisiana, we saw a fire along the road and no one was there putting it out. Guy had a broom and an old towel in the back of the truck, so we pulled over, got out and started beating out the brush fire. After a while, an elderly woman came down the hill and thanked us. She had seen the fire, but she said it always took a long time for the fire trucks to get there, and she was grateful we stopped. It seemed a strange event for a honeymoon.

We felt like life was a journey that we had just started as a couple---and if it was like this honeymoon, it would doubtless be an adventure with many surprises. And it has been, although some surprises were not as pleasant as we hoped. We never dreamed we would have such difficulties in having our own children. We are thankful for the two children we have on earth, and someday, we will meet the ones we have in Heaven.

Working with children was such a delight! In 1991, Guy left carpentry behind and became a full time children's pastor. Somehow, we just naturally became involved with puppetry.

This lasted until 2012, so we have been very blessed to enjoy that type of ministry so long. Sometimes I am sad, thinking about the children and the puppets, the costumes and the plays and all the excitement we had telling about Jesus with drama and action. I sit in my house by myself, and it is way too quiet.

Then the Lord reminds me that we are still on a journey, and He is still with me. He said He would never leave me, and He never has. He reminds me that we are still doing adventures, He and I----that we could not do with our busy former life. We have written and published books together, done portraits and photography, and written many devotionals.

Instead of preparing children's messages, I am preparing my heart for worship and prophecy and whatever the Lord wants to do in each service. He has been so gracious and kind to allow me to speak for Him, in a different way than I spoke to the children.

And who knows with Him? Perhaps there is a surprise just around the bend in the road.

"However, as the scripture says, "What no one ever saw or heard, what no one ever thought could happen, is the very thing God prepared for those who love him."
1 Corinthians 2:9 GNT

A MERRY HEART

Thanks, Lord

For making me laugh—

At myself.

Wrapped up in the dreary day

I didn't see the step---

Down I went.

On hands and knees in shredded hose,

And a crowd of people looking on.

I had to laugh.

It really cheers me up to know

That despite my somber, serious pose,

I'm still ridiculous.

"A happy heart is like good medicine, but a broken spirit
drains your strength." Proverbs 17:22 NCV

SALVATION

I heard the bells today
I lean toward them yearning
For more of His salvation
In my days
In my life
Their peace floats out to me
Over the swaying treetops
And catches me
On this balcony.
Their sound is fragrant on the air.
Like His words, they lift me
To a place untouched
By the busy clutter
Of the un-responding world.
The darkness, as he calls it,
Is the struggle and the turmoil
The churning grinding efforts
To accomplish, to recreate ourselves,
To make us right.
But when I heard His voice, my striving ceased.
His gentleness disarmed me
Made me surrender
To what I refused to believe.

And now I know why they say men are evil,

But God is good.

Who else but He can say "I am your strength,

Your sustenance, your source---lean on Me."

This is salvation.

"Trust in the LORD with all your heart
and lean not on your own understanding;
in all your ways submit to him,
and he will make your paths straight."

Proverbs 3:5-6

"By faith we understand that the universe was formed at God's command, so that what is seen was not made out of what was visible." Hebrews 11:3

He makes visible things out of the invisible.

He calls into existence the things that are not a reality yet.

"Though you have not seen him, you love him; and even though you do not see him now, you believe in him and are filled with an inexpressible and glorious joy, for you are receiving the end result of your faith, the salvation of your souls." 1 Peter 1:8-9

REFUTATION

You made everything that exists;

You created all the chemical

Equations in a molecule,

Thought up all the formulas----

All the things

That we've spent years

Discovering.

But----this guy in my class

Says writing about you

Is corny.

I'm really amazed---

You're still so polite

To him.

In my creative writing class at college, all of our poems were viewed by the other classmates, and subjected to critique or comments by the members of the class. This poem was my quiet rebuttal for the sarcastic remarks of another student in his poem, which were directed at my choice of subjects. I remember liking the guy for his candor, but I couldn't resist giving a mild rebuke for his arrogance, and I hoped to inject some humor into the otherwise tense feedback. I imagine he felt "safe" to bash God in such an avant-garde atmosphere as college, but thankfully the professor was a diplomatic sort of person and did not allow him to express antagonism. So I believe the "duel" ended in mutual respect; I didn't cower down, and he did not become hostile. I only wish I could have told him how much the Lord loves him.

YOU ARE DESIRABLE TO GOD

I think the attitude of the world—which is extremely critical, negative, and derogatory—combined with the devil's efforts, and the person's own misgivings, all work together against people to keep them from having any sense of value. God demonstrated how much He values us by sending His only Son to save us—-and the blood of Jesus was the unbelievable price He paid to redeem us.

"But God demonstrates his own love for us in this: While we were still sinners, Christ died for us." Romans 5:8

The more I see how personally Jesus loves us—each of us, even with all our personality quirks—the more it sets me free from any anxiety over who I am. He doesn't just tolerate us and have pity for us— He wants us close to Him always and desires our love—we are desirable to Him.

I can't get enough of His love! I long for more, and for others to experience this.

A CHANGE IN THE ATMOSPHERE

Lord, Your Word will outlast the earth.

In the beginning, Your Spirit hovered over the unformed earth and You brought order out of chaos. You created Light before there was ever a sun or moon or stars. How is this possible?

Nothing is impossible for You; the only thing that is impossible for you is nothing.

You are always doing something.

You are "an ever-present help in trouble." Psalm 46:1

At the dawn of creation, You merely said the word, and things came into existence.

This is the same Word that is sustaining us.

You said, "Heaven and earth will pass away, but my words will never pass away." Matthew 24:35

You are from everlasting to everlasting.

"You remain the same and your years will never end." Psalm 102:27

We trust in Your promises, that You will hear our cry and answer us.

You said that we could ask anything in your name and it would be done. John 14:14

Only one thing can stop the madness that is spreading across our nation, and that is Your Spirit, oh Lord. We ask You Lord to send a change in the "atmosphere" through the power of Your Spirit.

We ask for a revival of such magnitude that Your Light will dispel the darkness.

There is no other way, no other answer for the violence we have seen.

We will not allow Death to triumph; we will seek You for this Life to come.

We cry out for Your Spirit to come---move over our land.

Change the atmosphere by Your glory.

You are our refuge; we trust in Your Word.

You are the Life-giver; the only One who ever destroyed death.

We cry out to You.

"The eyes of the LORD are on the righteous,
and his ears are attentive to their cry;"

Psalm 34:15

"The righteous cry out, and the LORD hears them;
he delivers them from all their troubles."

Psalm 34:17

I HEARD HIS VOICE, BUT.....

I heard the Lord's voice, but I hesitated......

This happened when Guy and I had been married only a few years, and we didn't have any children yet. Guy had worked with several other men in a construction business of building houses, and then decided to start his own business. On this particular job, he was concerned that he might have underbid the cost of the house he was building, so he began to work extra hours alone, late at night. He hoped to speed up the progress so he wouldn't run out of payroll funds. (We were very new at this)

I had gotten used to the late night working sprees, so I went on to bed and fell asleep. After midnight one night, I suddenly woke up with the startling feeling that the Lord was telling me to get up and go to Loreauville. It was like I heard those words in my head.

But then there was silence....no other sign or indication that I was supposed to do this. I began to argue with myself over the rationality of doing this. I felt stupid and foolish for thinking such a crazy idea could be God's leading.

Back then, there were no cell phones; I don't think there were even cordless phones yet. At this time, I had another old hand-me-down vehicle, and this one was a big tank of a car with an 8 cylinder engine that gulped down gasoline.

The main problem was that I had only 1/8th of a tank of gas left, and Loreauville was about ten or so miles away, and it was in the middle of the night. No gas station between here and there would be open. Did I dare risk going?

I had just about talked myself out of it, when I thought again about the times I had heard the Lord's voice tell me to do something----especially when He woke me up out of a deep sleep. It just could not be a coincidence, so I finally convinced myself to get over the self-doubt and fear and just get in the car and go.

So about a half an hour or more had passed while I debated what I should do, when I finally began driving down that very dark road in the middle of the night.

As I got closer to the job site, I thought I spotted something moving along the side of the road----it looked like a person wearing a white T-shirt. I pulled over to get a closer look----- and it was Guy.

He had his knife pulled out because he didn't recognize the vehicle in the darkness.

His truck had stalled and wouldn't start, and there was no way to call me, so he began to pray. Finally, he started walking down the road. And that's where I found him.

I have since wondered why I hesitated like that---I think I had begun to doubt my ability to discern the Lord's voice.

If the enemy can convince us we are too stupid or unqualified to discern the Lord's voice, we won't take the risk to obey.....and someone's prayer goes unanswered or delayed----and someone you love may have to walk in the darkness for a while.

"..his sheep follow him because they know his voice."
John 10:4

MY KING

King of all Righteousness, King of all Peace
Under His rule, all war will cease.

Kingdoms of earth will rise and fall
His Kingdom alone will outlast them all.

From age to age, He remains the same
All authority is found within His name.

A priest forever, He ever lives
To intercede; His salvation He gives

To those who believe in the Blood that He shed
To those who believe in the Words that He said.

He gives us His love and calls us His bride
He is coming to take us to be at His side.

This will be rapture—to see His face
And at His table, to take our place.

Trust in His wisdom; when He is your king,
You will not lack any good thing.

No greater honor could He bestow
Than to give us His Spirit, His grace to show.

His Kingdom within us, the hope of His glory;
Our purpose it is to tell of His story.

That we will do, through the strength of His power.
So let us continue, for this is the hour.

A SINGER

I had a very unusual experience when our first child was born.

Our doctor sang during the delivery.

My first pregnancy ended in miscarriage, and the second one ended with heartbreak also. I lost that baby halfway through the pregnancy, and then we found out that the baby had a neural tube defect---anencephaly. Our doctor, Dr. Eugene Dauterive, grieved with us.

So when a healthy little girl was being born, he was singing!

Yesterday, I was singing to our little baby grandson, and he began to purse his lips and make sounds---and I realized this baby doesn't just want to talk; he wants to sing!

Recently, I was surprised and delighted to realize anew that the Lord is a singer.

"God sets the lonely in families, he leads out the prisoners with singing;" Psalm 68:6

"The Lord your God is with you, the Mighty Warrior who saves. He will take great delight in you; in his love he will no longer rebuke you, but will rejoice over you with singing." Zephaniah 3:17

Jesus sang with His disciples at the Last Supper. "When they had sung a hymn, they went out to the Mount of Olives." Matthew 26:30

No wonder it pleases Him when His people sing to Him.

Yesterday the church I was in began to have spontaneous worship singing; people began singing their own words of praise to the Lord with various intertwining harmonies.

The worship leader initiated this, and people began to join in with her. (myself included) The regular worship song with lyrics on the screen had ended, and then this began happening.

This singing was incredibly beautiful and the presence of the Lord was so magnificent. I went home as giddy and carefree as a little girl would be who just found out Jesus is real.

It was a taste of Heaven.

I think these Scriptures are referring to this phenomenon as "songs from the Spirit":

"speaking to one another with psalms, hymns, and songs from the Spirit. Sing and make music from your heart to the Lord," Ephesians 5:19

"Let the message of Christ dwell among you richly as you teach and admonish one another with all wisdom through psalms, hymns, and songs from the Spirit, singing to God with gratitude in your hearts." Colossians 3:16

THE KINGDOM

It's warm inside here---

Glowing faces

Warm embraces

Make me feel at ease---

Before us is a table spread with food---

Milk and honey and new wine;

The ointment flows down on our heads;

We are healed

As He is revealed

And the cold outside can't reach our hearts.

But we mourn for those outside

Like a mother for her child

Who's lost his way

In a snowstorm;

And the lantern's by the door

And we pray that they will see

Before the night comes.

BABYLON

Daniel was working among the academic elite of this nation, and yet he had a power that none of them possessed: the Spirit of God, who gave him supernatural abilities.

His little country of Israel had been overtaken by this monumental empire. And yet Daniel was able to believe in a kingdom far greater than this empire: the Kingdom of God.

Daniel faithfully served three kings of this earthly empire, because they were the authorities God had established. He was waiting for the time of the fulfillment of prophecy---when his people would see their homeland again.

Daniel never was able to return home, but he influenced the rulers of the mightiest empire on earth.

How did he do it?

Prayer.

"Evening, morning and noon
I cry out in distress, and he hears my voice."
Psalm 55:17

Courage comes from prayer:

"After they prayed, the place where they were meeting was shaken. And they were all filled with the Holy Spirit and spoke the word of God boldly." Acts 4:31

A SERVANT'S PRAYER

Lord, make my service as natural as breathing---

Like plants grow and flourish without any straining

And birds fly so high without any thinking.

Don't let me get sluggish and then fall asleep---

If You have to, then shake me

If You need to, then break me

Out of my lethargy into Your energy.

Give me sight for my blindness

And ears that can hear You

Make me sharp and perceptive,

Let Your love drive out fear.

Train my mind with Your Word,

Repel all my doubt--

Cure me of apathy, teach me Your strategy.

Fill me and fill me until Your love overflows

From a heart that is holy---

Like Yours.

HIS BLESSING

The blessings of God don't come to us because we are so special, or because we have earned "rank" in the Kingdom of God. They come to reveal the goodness of God, so that people will have hope and trust in the Lord.

The desire to scheme and manipulate to get what we want--- even in God's Kingdom---does not come from God. His Word tells us: "Take delight in the Lord, and he will give you the desires of your heart." Psalm 37:4 This is how fulfillment comes in the Kingdom of God.

Self-assertion, self-promotion, and self-reliance don't work in God's Kingdom.

After knowing the Lord for 45 years, I can look back and see how He has proved the truth of Psalm 37:4 to me in many ways. He is a faithful shepherd of our lives, and He personally teaches us His ways. I shudder to think of how awful it would have been to live without Him.

He kept me true to Him, all through college, despite a very worldly environment. He showered His grace on me through the loving fellowship and spiritual nourishment I received by being a part of Chi Alpha. College can be a cold-hearted place, but there was such warmth from the genuine faith and love at Chi Alpha.

In my senior year of college I was becoming concerned and depressed because of the major I was pursuing. I had chosen commercial art, thinking it would be a practical use of artistic abilities. Now I realized that most in this field would work in an advertising agency, and that didn't appeal to me at all. I suddenly had one of those "epiphany moments" when the Lord showed me that He had changed my desires, and that I really wanted to be a wife, a mother, and to work with children.

Not only did He change my desires, He then fulfilled them.

Here is how it happened: I went to see my pastor because of this uneasiness about my future decisions, and when he prayed for me, he started to cry. Then he prayed for something that was a terrifying thought to me! He asked the Lord to send my husband. I wasn't sure that I was ready for that life-changing adventure to begin right then!

The Lord answered the prayer of that godly pastor. The first Christian guy I ever met after I became a believer, showed up suddenly at a meeting. I had not seen him in several years, but that night he asked me to go with him to a church banquet. And so the adventure began....we were married the next year, and immediately began working with the children at church. We have loved working with children ever since.

I did finish with the art degree, although I changed the major to photography that last year instead of advertising design. That knowledge has proved helpful, even though it was film photography back then. The basic functions of a camera are still the same.

My dad always had a camera handy, so I guess it was a natural thing for me to like cameras.

My love for theater started at an early age, too. When I was a little girl, my mother brought my sister and I to see children's plays performed at the Casa Manana Theater in

Fort Worth. (We lived there) There was also a traveling group of actors who came and presented a play at my elementary school, and I was very excited about this.

I loved to read stories---I was an avid reader. When I saw that acting the stories out made them even more real to me, I thought that was so very awesome.

As a young adult, I saw the impact of acting out the stories of the Bible and Gospel truths. There was a traveling acting group who came to our church and presented a Christian children's play. They acted out the story called "Nathaniel the Grublet". (They were sponsored by a company that produced children's music.)

I was so impressed because when they gave the invitation at the end, to come to the front and receive Jesus as Savior, our two year old daughter responded! She asked to go to the front. I questioned her to be sure she understood what she was doing, and she told me that her Sunday School teacher had explained this to her. I don't remember who her teacher was at the time, but whoever you were, I appreciate you so much!! You planted the seed, someone else watered it, and God caused it to grow.

When our church performed "The Witness"----a musical story of the death and resurrection of Jesus----there were always commitments to Christ as a result. The whole church worked together for that outreach, and we developed bonds of love and comradeship through that. I think it always stirred our hearts, too, and made the Gospel more real to us as well.

So the Lord had given me the desire for acting, and then He fulfilled that desire through the ministries of our church.

Over the years, we did many children's dramas as a summer outreach, and did several original Christmas plays.

I think that the Lord's desire for us is that we would live very fulfilled lives built on His foundation. We may not look successful as far as the world's standards dictate, but the important thing is how we build on His foundation. 1 Corinthians 3:10-15

There was a prophecy that came immediately after the Supreme Court decision concerning the definition of marriage---and it showed how the Lord feels about the foundation of faith in our lives.

He said, "I will prove to you that My Word endures."

It does, and always will.

He is always true to His word.

"For the wisdom of this world is foolishness
in God's sight." 1 Corinthians 3:19

"For you have been born again, not of perishable seed,
but of imperishable, through the living and
enduring word of God."

1 Peter 1:23

OUR GOD

He made the Red Sea open and His people crossed;

The Rock gushed water as He said.

He sent them Heaven's bread when they were hungry;

Every single one of them was fed.

He led them with the cloud of His presence.

His fire was their shield at night.

For forty years of walking He provided for their feet

With shoes that endured their plight.

He made the giant city wall fall and crumble

At the sound of their single mighty shout

He held the Jordan River back from its flowing

They carried the river stones out.

He made the sun stand still for their army;

He turned back time for their quest.

When I see all these things together

How could I not rest?

In the knowledge of His wisdom and his care---

And that He alone knows best.

BY DESIGN

We can see God's designs all around us, in the things He created.

He brings order out of chaos, and beauty out of ashes.

He has designed each one of us, with a unique purpose in mind.

Not even two fingerprints are just alike, anywhere in the world or time.

We were created in God's image, according to His design.

But the design was corrupted by sin.

It's hard to even see the original design anymore.

But we can see it if we look at Jesus.

God's design and plan is to remake us like Him.

He knew us before we were born, and already had this plan for us!

"For those God foreknew he also predestined to be conformed to the image of his Son..."

Romans 8:29

A SURPRISE ENDING

I had never before seen a baby that looked like this; it was shocking.

And it was my own baby.

His head was the size of a lemon, his body the length of an ink pen, and his legs and feet were long and out of proportion to the rest of him, making him look like a frog.

I had gone into labor at 25 weeks, and he was born at 25 ½ weeks.

We became very acquainted with the Neonatal Intensive Care Unit. It was so hard to leave him there and go home. We came every day, but we were only allowed to stay a short time. I am so grateful to the nurses he had---they were very motherly and protective of him.

But he should have been in his own safe environment---the womb. Instead, he was out of it, and struggling to survive, covered in wires and hooked up to machines. We felt it would encourage him if he could hear our voices often, so we made a tape of ourselves singing, reading stories, and talking to him. We bought a tape player and speakers that were small enough to put in the incubator and the nurses let us leave it in there. He didn't take up much room, even in that---he was only 2 lbs. 2 oz.

One day when he was a little bigger---almost 3 lbs.----I walked into the NICU and was surprised to see him sitting up in an infant seat under the warming light. I didn't go up to him right away as I usually did; I stopped to ask the nurse if she would take a picture for me with the department's camera. Then I noticed something----his bottom lip was pushed out and was beginning to quiver. He was visibly upset. Babies can't see very well at that gestation, but he recognized my voice, and was unhappy that I didn't go right to him. He wanted his momma! The nurses also told me that they observed how much he responded to music.

Seeing his little personality develop there in the hospital made it ever so more clear to me of the horror of abortion. I could not bear the thought of babies bigger than him being horribly murdered and dismembered and thrown away....at the decision of their own mothers.

Abortion is a grisly barbaric act of violence; almost like cannibalism....it's taking a life to satisfy yourself. How did a civilized country become so barbaric that it is considered a legal right to murder your own child? America seems to be in such a stupor; how is it possible that we have allowed people in this nation to openly endorse killing babies? This is an unthinkable nightmare.

We were able to bring our baby home when he got up to 4½ lbs. God had spared his life, and also prevented any disabilities. We are so thankful for his life. He has now completed his undergraduate studies in college, and is going back to pursue his master's degree. I know that his life will make an impact on others---it already has.

It was a surprise ending to the pregnancy, but the beginning of the adventure of knowing another unique person created by God.

I wouldn't miss that for the world.

THE PARABLE

My life has become a parable---
A revealing story, an explicit tale;
Of the faithfulness of God---
And a Love that will not fail.

Time will reveal His intentions;
The beauty of an unsullied Grace.
The stumbling blocks meant for evil
Become milestones in this race.

His purposes not yet understood.
Will bring glory in the end;
The wonder, the marvel, the rapture
Of knowing the Lord as a friend.

And if I could but see
Into the future of His plan
I would know that we have been walking
Together, hand in hand.

BY THE SPIRIT

The enemy may accuse you of many things, but he cannot force Jesus to write you out of the Father's will!

The Lord's purposes remain firm and fixed, and no one can derail them.

When I was praying this morning, the Lord said, "There are no restrictions on Me."

"Surely the arm of the Lord is not too short to save, nor his ear too dull to hear." Isaiah 59:1

No one can keep you from the heritage the Lord has for you: the heritage of the Holy Spirit.

"Peter replied, 'Repent and be baptized, every one of you, in the name of Jesus Christ for the forgiveness of your sins. And you will receive the gift of the Holy Spirit. The promise is for you and your children and for all who are far off—for all whom the Lord our God will call.'" Acts 2:38-39

The battles we face are won "not by might, nor by power, but by my Spirit, says the Lord almighty." Zechariah 4:6

"no weapon forged against you will prevail,
and you will refute every tongue that accuses you.
This is the heritage of the servants of the Lord,
and this is their vindication from me,"
declares the Lord." Isaiah 54:17

THE UNEXPECTED

Not long ago, I found myself in the emergency room of the hospital, with symptoms of a heart attack. The chest pain happened so suddenly and was so severe, that the only thing to do was to get to the hospital. This was certainly not what I planned to do that day.

An EKG, a chest X-ray, and bloodwork, revealed there was nothing wrong with my heart, thank God. In fact, all the tests showed that I am in remarkably good health!

It turned out to be a strange muscle problem that causes inflammation of the chest wall. I think the clinical term is "costochondritis", and the pain mimics a heart attack. After a shot for the pain took effect, I was ready to go home.

When faced with the prospects of a heart attack, I realized a few things: I wasn't afraid. If I left here, I know I would be in the presence of the Lord, and that would be so wonderful!

However, I didn't want to leave a vacancy of wife, mother, and grandmother. I didn't want to cause that grief and loss for my family. Also, I was disappointed at the thought that I didn't get to do Ruby's portrait or write the sequel to the children's book I recently published.

More importantly, I did not want to miss out on helping with the revival I believe the Lord is going to send. I want to complete every assignment the Lord chooses to give me!

I'm glad I have this time to do things for the Kingdom of God and be a part of His harvest. I thought about this Scripture: "My times are in your hands" from Psalm 31:15

There are things I have prayed for that have not been answered yet; I am waiting. I thought about Simeon who was waiting to see the fulfillment of God's promises.

"It had been revealed to him by the Holy Spirit that he would not die before he had seen the Lord's Messiah. Moved by the Spirit, he went into the temple courts. When the parents brought in the child Jesus to do for him what the custom of the Law required, Simeon took him in his arms and praised God, saying: "Sovereign Lord, as you have promised, you may now dismiss your servant in peace. For my eyes have seen your salvation, which you have prepared in the sight of all nations: a light for revelation to the Gentiles and the glory of your people Israel." Luke 2:26-32

I pray I will be prompted by the Holy Spirit as Simeon was; that I will respond and obey so that I will be in the right place at the right time, for the fulfillment of God's plan in my life.

Lord, what You are doing is beyond the scope of my imagination and understanding. Help me not to be discouraged even when it seems like nothing at all is happening---even when it seems like I am doing nothing worthwhile. You are my timekeeper.

We don't even know what will happen tomorrow, but He does. James 4:13-15

Our times are in His hands.

*(The Lord enabled me to write the sequel
to the children's book, and I am very grateful!)*

IN HIS BOOK

There's an expression called "in my book". It means "In my opinion; from my perspective." In His book, you can see the Lord's perspective.

In His book, love means:

Passion for His kingdom,

Commitment to His word,

Surrender to His will,

Caring for the helpless, and

Loving His family as our own.

His name is written all over His book; He signed His name with His own blood.

It's a priceless "first edition autographed book" given to you and me from Jesus.

Read it every day to see His viewpoint.

"Then I said, Look, I have come.
It is written about me in the book."

Psalm 40:7 NCV

WORSHIP THE LORD

You say I'm foolish

That I need to repent

Because I poured out all my tears

On his feet---

You think it proper

To have a rite

A ritual, religion----

But my joy you call unlawful.

I'm in love with my God!

Like a bride in white,

I'm not ashamed

To take His name;

To lift my hands

In adoration.

You think the cripple didn't

Leap and shout

When He touched him?

Why should I do any less?

This poem is written in reference to the woman who wept on Jesus' feet, wiped them with her hair, and poured perfume on his feet and head.

Luke 7:36-38, Mark 14:3-4, Matthew 26:6-13

The religious society who witnessed this looked down on her with scorn and contempt and reviled her.

They were disgusted and embarrassed by her undignified, unseemly display of emotion. She did not care; she had lived an utterly sinful life and was well acquainted with shame and degradation.

What could compare with having ALL your sins forgiven and being accepted by God? Nothing. All the money in the world could not buy that.

No one in her life had ever done anything like this for her or treated her with so much respect.

The people watching this lavish display criticized her for wasting the perfume, but the Lord commended her.

This woman appreciated His sacrifice to rescue her from sin more than any there that day, and Jesus appreciated hers.

With our heartfelt expressive worship, we too can show our appreciation for His forgiveness.

Remember the alabaster jar....
break yourself open and pour out your praise.

MY TREASURE BOX

Everyone in my family has a treasure box of some sort. My husband Guy has one that looks like a teakwood box made in India with carving on top, our son has my old Lane miniature replica cedar chest, and I have one that looks like a small wooden trunk with leather straps. We each have our mementos and memorabilia stashed away for safe keeping in our treasure boxes.

I have an invisible "treasure box" also---and I'm sure you do, too. It's filled with memories. There aren't many from high school days that I take out and look at----high school was such a jungle of carnivorous attitudes, and I just tried to survive. But there are a few....

There was the time that one of my friends expressed disgust that she was described as "kind." She thought kindness was a bland, lame, wimpy thing to be remembered for. I didn't say anything (my default position) but I remember thinking that in our cruel world of high school hate, having the courage to be kind was a great accomplishment indeed.

Then there was the time in my English class that I broke out of my silence, and the whole class was in shock! The only time I was quite vocal was in drama class---I had no problem expressing myself then. But in a regular class setting, I gave no feedback whatsoever. I became the girl with no voice.

Our reading assignment was The Pearl by John Steinbeck, and we each had our own paperback copy of the book. Somehow, with my pencil eraser, I removed parts of the letters and shaped others until the title was no longer The Pearl. It was....The Bean.

When I showed it to my friend, we couldn't hold it back----we burst out laughing. I have a cackle that tends to make other people laugh, and the whole class was laughing with us when they saw the book. Even our teacher couldn't help herself and she was laughing.

I wish I had kept that copy of the book! I don't remember what happened to it---maybe I gave it to my friend, and it's in her treasure box. I still laugh when I think about The Bean.

Did you ever feel as if your life is like that? You started out with a pearl in your treasure box, but then one day you opened it, and it's not a pearl----it's a bean.

Someone erased parts of you, and your title is changed. You don't have the same value anymore. You might start feeling very sorry for yourself, except that suddenly you realize something----a bean could be a seed. You can plant it, and grow living things. Your life can still produce nourishment; the potential is still there.

The greatest treasure you could have can never be taken away or erased from your life. This is the Kingdom of God----the pearl of great price. The Kingdom of God is of such tremendous value that nothing can be compared to it. And it can be yours----forever. What is the cost of such a treasure to obtain it? You----your life. Be prepared to give away your life; but when you meet Jesus and He becomes the loving ruler of your heart, there is nothing worth more than His Kingdom. Matthew 13:44-45

"But seek first his kingdom..." Matthew 6:33

THE JEWS

God's children rejected their brother
Born in the city of David
Under the star of David
Born of the seed of David
He was a Jew.

I am just an adopted daughter
Born of the Gentile race
But I hear your children crying
I hear the prophets crying
Oh, Israel.

Oh, Lord, redeem your people
For David saw them scattered
And their slaughter in the war
And their name as just a byword
Among the heathen.

Oh, Lord, redeem your people,
For they are down at the wailing wall,
Crying for their Messiah
Still waiting for their Messiah
Who has already come.

JESUS WAS A JEW

Sometimes people forget that Jesus was a Jew. He spoke in Hebrew, and He followed Jewish customs. Many of the parables and things that He said, relate to Jewish culture.

Since Jesus has adopted us into His family when we accept His sacrifice, the Jewish people become our family, too.

I am so thrilled when I read the testimonies of Jewish people who have come to believe in Jesus as their Messiah.

The heritage of faith belonged to them first.

I am so grateful for the Scriptures that have come to us through the Jewish people. We have been blessed through them in many ways. They are a sign to the world of the truth of God's Word.

"Remember that in the past you were without Christ. You were not citizens of Israel, and you had no part in the agreements with the promise that God made to his people. You had no hope, and you did not know God. But now in Christ Jesus, you who were far away from God are brought near through the blood of Christ's death. Christ himself is our peace. He made both Jewish people and those who are not Jews one people. They were separated as if there were a wall between them, but Christ broke down that wall of hate by giving his own body. The Jewish law had many commands and rules, but Christ ended that law. His purpose was to make the two groups of people become one new people in him and in this way make peace."
Ephesians 2:12-15 NCV

A FUNNY THING HAPPENED

When my family migrated from Texas to Louisiana in 1965, we were not acquainted with hurricanes. We were more familiar with the threat of tornados, dust storms, and the Cuban missile crisis. After we were settled in Louisiana, we saw the winds of Hurricane Betsy, but we didn't see a lot of damage other than a few trees knocked down. So in my ten-year-old mind, the hurricane danger seemed like hype. We children were mostly interested in getting a holiday from schoolwork.

South Louisiana was spared from any very destructive storms for a number of years, it seems. And I had the better sense to be grateful for that trend, and that it lasted as long as it did. Every tropical storm that DIDN'T become a hurricane was a cause for rejoicing.

Then we got more acquainted with storms.

In 1992, Hurricane Andrew took the roof off of our school.

In 2002, Hurricane Lili took the roof off of our church.

Then came the maelstrom of Hurricane Katrina in 2005, with Hurricane Rita following on its heels. Family members and friends were severely affected by these storms.

So when Hurricane Gustav threatened in 2008, we headed for Texas. My sister's place barely gets enough rain, much less hurricanes. So we thought it would be a vacation of sorts, and an opportunity to visit with my sister and her family, as well.

And it was. I can't say we "chilled" because it was very hot and dry! But we did relax---you can't move very fast in that kind of heat---it feels like slow motion. We helped out at my sister's---Guy mowed the grass; (what little there was) and I weeded the garden, (whatever was left after the deer ate their favorites) and Isaac watched Disney movies like "Holes".

And about every other day, we made the usual trek to the small town Walmart. That's when the crazy stuff started happening.

(Why does it always follow the Lavergnes?----like the time we went to Florida and it snowed?)

Anyway, every time we went through the Walmart entrance, their store alarm went off.

Now, you need to know that my sister's husband was a law enforcement officer at that time----and he was very embarrassed at walking through those doors with people who set off the alarm!

The store manager tried to help us solve the mystery.

(After about the second or third time, my sister's husband was nowhere near when we walked through---he had disappeared.)

Each time, the manager had Guy take off something and try going through the door: his watch, then his belt, then everything in his pockets, and so on. Nothing worked..... and the alarm continued to go off.

Finally, about the next to last day of our stay, we walked through those Walmart doors, and the inevitable alarm went off, but this time the manager had a brainstorm. He passed his "scanner" device (that could deactivate theft-prevention implants) over Guy's brown shoes. It was the shoes!

Guy had bought them in our hometown Walmart TWO years before, but they triggered something in this Texas store.

Well, that was a relief.

That night, we all went out to eat at a Chinese restaurant.

After the meal, we opened our fortune cookies, and guess what Guy's message was? "You need some new shoes."

We laughed so hysterically that tears were running out of my eyes. I love the fact that the Lord has such a sense of humor.

Then my sister's husband suggested we go back to Walmart so he could buy Guy some new shoes. But Guy liked his old brown ones, even if they did make him look like a criminal!

And so goes another saga in Lavergne vacations.

"Have mercy on me, my God, have mercy on me,
for in you I take refuge.
I will take refuge in the shadow of your wings
until the disaster has passed."

Psalm 57:1

NO LONGER THERE

She saw the horror of an unjust crime;
A guiltless man was forced to die.
His body was wrapped and hastily stored
In a cave nearby.

Sealed with a stone, and secured by guards,
No one could enter that night.
Yet the strangest scene awaited her
In the morning light.

The soldiers were gone and the stone pushed aside--
Someone had broken in.
Though frightened of what she might find,
She had to look within.

Dismay and grief tore at her heart
As she viewed his burial place.
They had ravaged his tomb and removed him!
His body was disgraced.

They hated him without a cause!
And defiled him while she slept.
There was nothing she could do for him,
And so she wept.

She saw a man in the garden there--
This was the least that she could do;
She begged him to tell where the body was,
If only he knew.

He said her name, and her heart nearly stopped.
Only one voice could sound like this;
Only one voice was Heaven speaking;
And it was His.

"Go back and tell my brothers I am alive", he said.
"And they will soon see that it is true.
For all that has happened is fulfilling God's Word,
Just as I told you."

And as He gently pried her hands from him,
She saw His kind smile through her tears.
He said, "I have a meeting with my Father now,
But have no fears."

"He is now your Father too as well.
Through my blood, you have His love.
There will be a place prepared for you
In His home above."

"I will stay here only a little while longer,
And then I must go away.
The Holy Spirit will come and comfort you
Until that day,

When my Father says the time has come
For the marriage banquet to take place,
I will call you and take you to my side--
You will see my face.

There are others who I want there;
You must tell them this for me.
Our separation will forever end; for where I am,
You will be."

Maranatha! Come Lord Jesus!

This poem shows how Mary misunderstood what was happening----like all the disciples, she could not comprehend the meaning of the circumstances that she saw developing around her.

She treasured the Lord so much, and felt such intense grief at all that had happened to Him. But her grief turned to joy at the surprise appearance of Jesus. And what He said to her---and to all of us---shows the magnitude of His love for us, and His attraction to us.

He wants us to be with Him, and see His glory----He is waiting for that day!

John 13-17 and 20

A VERY INTENSE DREAM

In 2008, I had a vivid dream that I have never forgotten because in that dream I heard the Lord's voice, though I did not see Him.

In my dream, I was digging---and that wasn't too unusual because recently I had been doing a lot of gardening, and digging up the flower beds.

But then I heard the Lord's voice coming from behind me, and He sounded like a parent who is gently correcting a child. He said, "What are you doing?"

And I answered very sheepishly, "I'm scared of the talent You gave me." And then I woke up.

I knew immediately this corresponded to His parable of the talents. (Matthew 25) I did NOT want to be anything like the servant who dug a hole and buried the talent.

That servant did not want to obey the Lord and invest his energy in the Kingdom of God because he had the wrong idea about the Lord. He didn't realize how good the Lord is to His servants; he thought of the Lord as a harsh, hard, mean master.

I did not want to sabotage my relationship with the Lord by mistrusting Him as that servant did.

At the time, we were preparing for an evangelical outreach-- a children's theater production---and I was nervous about the enormity of doing that production.

I didn't feel all that qualified or confident about my abilities to direct a large production, and as usual there were many obstacles.

But after that dream, there was NO way I would back out!!

With the help of a large team of enthusiastic people, and the Lord's grace, we accomplished it, and I will never regret that endeavor.

I still pray about the message in that dream.....I want to be sure I complete all His assignments!

With every talent that He gives, comes a responsibility---they are meant to be used to bless others and further the Kingdom of God.

Yes, the Lord DOES speak to us....sometimes in very unusual ways.

"Then a great and powerful wind tore the mountains apart and shattered the rocks before the LORD, but the LORD was not in the wind. After the wind there was an earthquake, but the LORD was not in the earthquake. After the earthquake came a fire, but the LORD was not in the fire. And after the fire came a gentle whisper. When Elijah heard it, he pulled his cloak over his face and went out and stood at the mouth of the cave.

Then a voice said to him, "What are you doing here, Elijah?"

1 Kings 19:11-13

HIS FACE

Picture the Lord standing in front of you.

He is looking at you lovingly.

If you want to hear His voice, let Him hear yours.

Sing to Him---sing a love song to Him.

Pour out your heart to Him.

When you begin to passionately seek Him,

you will begin to feel His passion for you.

And you will want more---

and He wants more of you, too.

"My heart says of you, "Seek his face!"
Your face, Lord, I will seek." Psalm 27:8

"Let your face shine on your servant;
save me in your unfailing love."

Psalm 31:16

THE RESCUE

You number the stars; You gave each a name.

Though their light may fade, You remain the same.

Your glory is seen in the Heavens above

Your compassion is felt in Your eternal love.

And Love has a name; this love became man.

Though He existed as God before time began.

No mortal has witnessed a greater plan

Than the one He enacted to rescue man.

His blood was spilled, His life ebbed away—

On a wooden cross, He died that day.

And some would spurn, and some would jeer,

But those who believed died without fear.

So come and rejoice, and forget your loss;

All has been found at the foot of the Cross.

And none should despair, for His grace is free;

We are made rich through His poverty.

His favor bestowed, His righteousness shared,

He gives us His strength; in suffering He cared.

More than we know, His love met our need—

Mercy after mercy, we have received.

So call Him your Savior and take up His name—

As your rightful owner—no longer to blame

For the evil of mankind, or the cause of pain---

But the Giver of Life, that is His name.

How incredible---what a wonder it is to realize that the God who created the heavens and all its galaxies would want my praise---and yours---that He would desire our love so much that He would become human and go through all that He did.

Compared to the heavens---the moon and the stars and the reaches of space---of what consequence are humans? Yet He wants us to know Him and He wants us to be with Him so much that He left Heaven to come and die.

There is no greater love. I want to see Him and be with Him for I have never known a love like His; a love that prizes me the way He does, though I have no merit of my own.

.

"He determines the number of the stars
and calls them each by name." Psalm 147:4

MUD

When our son started college, my husband and I purposed to help him with his tuition for four years. Our state provided a scholarship fund at the time, which would help cover a large portion of his tuition. Thankfully, the college close by us had lower rates of tuition than most institutions. So each semester, we were able to provide one fourth of the tuition, and the rest was covered by the scholarship fund. We praised God for this provision.

However, the last semester of the fourth year, something changed.

The scholarship funds had been slowly dwindling and decreasing with each semester, and by the time we got to this eighth one, only one fourth of the tuition was covered.

We needed three-fourths of the amount, which was about $3500.

Our son was feeling panicky; he had not seen many miracles of provision, so he was not used to having to believe for this.

I felt that it was a wonderful opportunity to experience a miracle, and told him that we would pray and believe that the Lord would provide.

He was somewhat skeptical of this, having become a very "wise" college student by now!

Yet the Lord answered prayer, in the most unusual way.

There was some family property in another part of the state, on which there was a small oil well. We received a small (very small) royalty off and on throughout the year. Finally, we received notice that the well would be shutting down; it was no longer productive enough to keep it in operation.

The company had a small problem; they needed a place to spread the mud left from drilling. They asked for permission to spread it on some of the family property.

Some of the family members dissented to this, but we agreed to let them spread it on our part of the property. In return, the oil company compensated us monetarily for that privilege.

The amount of the check came out to about $3500.

I laugh now when I tell the story; God answered with mud! Who else would have thought of that? It sounds just like something the Lord would do.

He sent Peter to go fishing when they needed a little extra to pay their taxes and they didn't have it. Peter was instructed to open the mouth of the first fish he caught, and he would find what he needed. Sure enough, there was a coin in the mouth of the fish Peter caught.

And our college student saw a miracle, too.

"And my God will meet all your needs
according to the riches of his glory in Christ Jesus."
Philippians 4:19

LOVE IS GIVING

Lord, you gave

And you still do

You give and give

And keep on giving

Like the oil that wouldn't run out

In the widow's vessels.

But selfishness

Is a brand of the antichrist

A mark of the Beast;

That practical sort of self-preservation

That holds back for oneself.

Let me be foolish, then

For your sake---and theirs'

For You'll turn it

Into Wisdom.

"God gives the Spirit without limit." John 3:34

HIS FLOCK

We are all weak; we are only sheep. Our strength comes from Christ alone, so that no one can look down on anyone else. Apart from Christ, we can do NOTHING.

We cannot allow ourselves to become arrogant sheep, after we observe how tenderly and lovingly the Lord washed the feet of His friends.

Don't gloat or despise anyone for their weakness, or the Lord's heart will be grieved. Strengthen them and nourish them with the comfort God has given you in your own weakness. He treats us like His beloved children, and no one is rejected who comes to Him.

Let confidence come from His anointing and not from the strength of human personality. Then He will receive the glory.

Lord, help us live in Your capabilities and not our own.

Bury me in Your love, Lord, and let me live by Your resurrection power.

"I have been crucified with Christ
and I no longer live, but Christ lives in me.
The life I now live in the body, I live by faith
in the Son of God, who loved me and gave himself for me."

Galatians 2:20

THAT CALL

We got a phone call from the sheriff's department in the middle of the night. You can imagine our first thought. The sheriff doesn't usually call like that unless there has been a terrible accident.

The last time we had spoken to our son Isaac was about 11:30 that night. He and another employee at our church were moving chairs used in the school gym for an event, back over to the church building for school on Monday. (the fellowship hall is also the school cafeteria) He was almost finished then, and would be heading home soon.

Then we were awakened by this call at 1:00 a.m. The sheriff's representative calling on my phone asked to speak to my husband Guy.

What happened is this: A large group of law enforcement officers converged on the two young men, right outside the gym as they were locking the doors. The officers were fully armed and aimed, and were shouting commands at them.

Isaac complied with everything they said, including handcuffs, and then calmly explained what they were doing and why.

That is why we got the phone call---they were asking Guy to verify Isaac's explanation.

I am very thankful for our law enforcement officers who work to protect us and our properties. We know the officers thought this school incident was a break-in, and didn't know the young men were actually working. The officers were doing their job.

It's another reminder to pray for our city government---these people are our neighbors, friends, and relatives.

So we had a very eventful weekend----we had our granddaughter with us on Saturday, we found abandoned newborn kittens in our yard and tried to save them, our dog had diarrhea, the cat got in it and we had to bathe her, and Isaac almost got arrested for moving chairs.

The Lavergne weekend can sometimes get very interesting!

"I urge, then, first of all,
that petitions, prayers, intercession
and thanksgiving be made for all people—
for kings and all those in authority,
that we may live peaceful and quiet lives
in all godliness and holiness.
This is good, and pleases God our Savior,
who wants all people to be saved
and to come to a knowledge of the truth."

1 Timothy 2:1-4

THE DAY LOVE DIED

The day love died, it broke my heart---

I never cried like this before.

To see Him hanging on the cross---

To realize my great loss;

He took my guilt, he bore my shame;

And I will never be the same.

It took an awesome act of God

To make me right with Him.

But evil could not conquer love---

His work was not yet done.

In His love, God's glory shone---

A brilliant light, an earthquake roar---

Love has come alive once more!

Love will never die again;

He's won the victory over sin.

I've entrusted everything to Love;

He's worthy of it all.

He said he has a task for me;

And I will heed His call.

The day Love died,

He gave Himself for me.

He rose again---

Now Love's alive in me.

"Who do people say I am?" Jesus asked His disciples. What people think he is, is not who He is.

He is who God says he is---God said, "This is my beloved Son."

Who do people say you are? It may not be accurate. You are who the Lord says you are.

The Heavenly Father revealed to Peter that Jesus was the Christ. It is who the Father says you are that really matters.

What He reveals is the truth. Matthew 16:13-18

People may appreciate what you do, and yet not appreciate who you are.

The Lord is not like this. He loves us for who we are, not for what we do.

SHOES

We suddenly detected a smell in the house....and then began the frantic sniffing search for the culprit. Whose shoe brought this undesirable odor into our house?

The main detective activity at our house is sniffing shoes.

We don't usually have to search for any missing shoes. I remember one year at kids' camp when a girl kicked off her shoe, and we didn't find it until the end of the week!! That missing shoe did not trouble her at all. She just borrowed someone else's.

It's not like that at our house---no, all of our shoes are paired with their sole mate every day and night. Guy even ties the shoelaces together!

We have two dogs, so there are booby traps in the yard for shoes. How dare you even think of wearing those shoes with millions of tiny grooves in the bottom when you go into the dog yard! There is a collection of old toothbrushes for this dilemma....

(At our house, we don't wash each other's feet-----we clean each other's shoes.)

So the house rule is: please pay attention when you put your foot down ....and check your shoes before you walk into the house. Be careful about where and how you are walking, and remove anything offensive before you spread it everywhere.

It's a good life rule, too.

We want to have the good fragrance of Christ in our home---our prayers are like incense, which gives off a good fragrance. Revelation 5:8

Also, wear the shoes of peace---the ones that spread the Good News.

Goodness smells good to those who are searching.

"Our offering to God is this:
We are the sweet smell of Christ
among those who are being saved
and among those who are being lost."

2 Corinthians 2:15 NCV

"Follow God's example, therefore, as dearly loved children and walk in the way of love, just as Christ loved us and gave himself up for us as a fragrant offering and sacrifice to God."

Ephesians 5:1-2

"For shoes, put on the peace that comes from the Good News so that you will be fully prepared."

Ephesians 6:15 NLT

ATMOSPHERE

The good taste of Heaven was in that place;

The love of Christ like healing waves

Flowed over us.

And our doubts melted, our fears fled---

Pain was dissolved; and hunger was fed:

By the Bread of Life who feeds us all,

No matter how few or many.

Tears of joy washed my face,

Streaming down unhindered---

As His kindness and His gracious love,

Covered me.

How then can you ask

Is it worth the time we spend?

To bask in His mercy and feel it erase

The effects of unloving rejection---

An end to the struggle of life purpose lost,

Found once again in His story---

The marvel of hope in His wonderful peace,

In his name the treasure of glory!

A thousand times yes! I will say it again---

It is worth it.

Look to the Lord and live!

Focus on Him and thrive.

Life is in Him.

Apart from Him, you can do nothing.

Yield to the Holy Spirit.

That means He has the right-of-way to move.

The enemy is trying to squeeze the life out of you.

Resist him in the authority of the name of Jesus.

Religion represses the voice of God.

Jesus is saying,

"But whoever listens to me will have security.

He will be safe, with no reason to be afraid."

Proverbs 1:33 GNT

Jesus says, "The thief comes only to steal and kill

and destroy; I have come that they may have life, and

have it to the full." John 10:10

THE ANSWER

Years ago, our former pastor, Rev. Don Neel, had a dream of starting a Christian school. He enlisted the help of Rev. and Mrs. Marvin Davenport, and the dream became a reality.

Both of our children graduated from this school, and we have never regretted investing in the financial amount needed for this endeavor. The willing hearts of God's people gave to this, and today the school is still active and flourishing.

About thirty years ago, there were so many kindergarteners registered that a second teacher was needed. (Most grades had only one class) I learned about this need that summer, and so I was praying for the school administration.

I was earnestly praying about this because someone had asked me to, and also because I had been teaching the pre-K four old children several mornings a week at the church. Many of my former students would be advancing to Kindergarten, and they would be placed in the extra Kindergarten class.

I remember that I was on my knees by the sofa, asking the Lord to send just the right person for this teaching position.

Much to my surprise, I heard the Lord answer me in this way: "I am. It's you."

It was so clear in my mind, that I knew it was Him. Still, I was frightened because I realized that some people would think I was not qualified since my college degree is in fine arts and not in education.

Scary or not, I knew I had to apply for the job.

I ended up teaching that year and the next, and I loved teaching kindergarten! It was so exciting to see their development and progress in reading and math and social skills. They were like my children. (My own daughter was about the same age at that time, too.)

After that second year, my husband asked me to give it up, and I cried. I thought I had found my niche in teaching kindergarten, but he felt the commitment needed to obtain a teaching certificate would result in a hardship on our family. Deep inside, I knew he was right, so I reluctantly resigned.

I was back to praying for God's next direction.

About a year later, the Lord answered. Our pastor, Rev. Paul Neel, asked my husband and I to join the staff at church as the children's pastors and elementary chaplains at the school.

We did that for twenty-one years and loved it.

With every new assignment, I have had to seek the Lord for boldness to step out in faith; but He is faithful to answer.

"When I called, you answered me;
you greatly emboldened me."

Psalm 138:3

THE SIGHT OF BARTIMAEUS

I sat there by the roadside, abandoned in my lack.

Disadvantaged by affliction, and without a hope for change,

I had no place but this.

I listened to the voices of the travelers who passed.

I could not see their faces, and it always seemed as though

Their words were distant in my ears.

One day there was commotion—many footsteps on the path.

I begged and pleaded for the answer from those who passed me by,

Who is it that is coming on this way?

When I heard His name, I shouted and a hope began to rise,

Some decried me and denied me, but I shouted all the more

Jesus, Son of David, hear my plea!

Those who had deplored me changed their favor at His word.

"He's calling you," they told me---then up I leaped and went to Him.

I knelt there at His feet.

"What is it that you want?" He asked, and then I told Him "Sight."

And when He gave it to me, then these eyes of mine could see His face---

I followed Him that day.

He went into Jerusalem and taught us in the Temple Courts.

After that I couldn't find Him; He had gone away somewhere to pray.

Then at last I saw Him.

Oh, these wretched eyes of mine! --- to be healed in time to see Him die.

My joy had brought to me such grief--- my only hope was crucified

And sealed up in a tomb.

Then what strange tales the women told us! They said He was alive;

Would my eyes behold His form again----or was it but a dream?

I could not surmise.

I stayed as close as possible to all His friends I knew, and hoped for just one glimpse---

Just in case it could be true, that He would come and find us,

And show Himself to us.

That day He did is marked upon my mind; and it cannot be erased.

With these very eyes of mine, I have seen the Hope of Glory!

He is Alive.

REAL

The God who created the universe spent 33 years with us as one of us.

This is more wonderful, more amazing, more fantastic than any fable or fairy tale that mankind has ever invented or imagined.

In the lives of young adults, the enemy does his utmost to make it seem just that: a fairy tale that they have outgrown.

He tries to substitute his own reality: a world without faith or obedience.

This world is so saturated with doubt and unbelief and we have grown so accustomed to it, that we assume it is normal and natural.

It is the lies we have lived with, that make up the unnatural state.

God is as real as the stars and the flowers that He created for us---and His Word is as true as Himself.

The only thing that will break through the atmosphere of unbelief is a complete surrender to Him.

It is the only way to begin seeing His story as the Real one.

THANKSGIVING AT THE LAVERGNE'S

It was a perfect day, until…..

Wait, let me "set the stage" for you.

We had a quiet day at home; our guest of honor was Guy's brother Perry. We had our turkey and our dressing, cranberry sauce, sweet potatoes, and the rest…and during the meal we talked about that first Thanksgiving long ago.

Later in the afternoon, we decided to rearrange the furniture to set up our 8 foot Christmas tree. In our small parlor, that is an engineering feat! We succeeded in coming up with an arrangement, so we were glad over that.

Then it happened. A bird had pooped on Guy's shirt earlier; so that evening, I proceeded to wash a load of clothes. A little while later, Guy came to the computer room to tell me that the kitchen was flooded! And it was….about a third of it was covered with almost an inch of water. We were very alarmed, not knowing the cause. Then Guy realized that the washing machine hose was not reconnected properly….and he became Charlie Brown because he knew it was his fault. Thankfully, I did not become Lucy. ("You blockhead!")

Instead, I laughed…..at the irony of the situation! We spent our Thanksgiving evening soaking up water with old towels and blankets.

I laughed because I remembered another Lavergne Thanksgiving. It was 2006, and we went to Disneyworld as a family for the first time ever. The welcome center had previously told me that it is ALWAYS 70 degree weather there, so only bring spring/summer clothing. So we did.

And guess what? Florida had freak weather that Thanksgiving, and it snowed! We went to the store to buy coats, and they had none. So we layered! (Forget style; we wore anything and everything over all that we had) It was so cold, and when we got home, Isaac's cough turned into mild pneumonia. But that's not what we remember most; we remember how we laughed about the snow! It was just so ironic....so fitting for a Lavergne Thanksgiving. And we had fun, despite the lack of suitable clothing.

Back to this year....well, that bird started it all!

I wish I could say that I always laughed my way through stressful situations, but at least this one, I did.

This morning, I read this:

"The Lord delights in those who fear him, who put their hope in his unfailing love." Psalm 147:11.

You know how your children (and grandchildren!) make you laugh?

I hope I make Him laugh!

"happy are the people whose God is the Lord."

Psalm 144:15 NCV

THE ROAD TO EMMAUS

My heart was utterly broken--
And all my hopes had died.
The man we thought our Savior
The Romans crucified.

We walked along the road to home,
Our eyes unfocused gazed.
We spoke of our desolation
And the loss of hopes he raised.

He healed the sick and raised the dead,
But his life he could not save.
We hid like rabbits in a burrow,
No longer were we brave.

And then we met the stranger
As we journeyed on our way.
He knew nothing of the sad events
Of that dreadful day.

We told him of our sorrow,
But he told a different tale;
How the Scriptures show a marvelous truth---
That God's plan did not fail.

In our hearts, we sensed a burning
And our souls began to heal.
When he spoke, God's Word became alive
And its meaning very real.

Then he shared a meal with us,
And when he divided up the bread,
Suddenly---we realized who he was;
The man we thought was dead.

Then he vanished from our sight.
We went back the way we came.
We had to tell that this had happened---
Now nothing was the same.

And while we met with friends in secret,
He suddenly appeared!
He let us touch his hands and feet,
His side the soldier speared.

His love began to fill the room and all our hearts as well.
Then we knew what he had done.
He broke the power of sin and death—
Our salvation he has won.

These scars he bears on his body,
That he showed to us so freely,
Are the symbols of what we mean to him---
Throughout Eternity.

THIS HOUSE

I'm grateful for this house I live in, even though sometimes it didn't meet my expectations.

Take sports, for instance: the only game I really enjoyed playing was badminton, because any ball ever used always seemed to connect with me at the wrong place!

Then in my teen years, there was the issue of the monthly female obligation. I had such painful times that it would make me throw up. One old family doctor said it was all in my mind. Later, after going through the first stages of labor and delivery and comparing the similarities between the two, I can definitely say, "Nope. I did not think that up!"

It was a muscle contraction, not a mental aberration.

Then there was the back of the house; it never seemed very sturdy. I don't know if it was the effect of the car wreck I was in as a child, (we only had lap belts and no shoulder belts) a case of mild scoliosis, ignorant misuse, or a combination of all of these.

The result was that the cushion between the spinal bones got out of place and was being pushy. That really got on my nerves, so half of the cushion had to be removed.

There went part of the shock absorber for bumpy rides, so now I must avoid riding bicycles, horses, and buses.

When I got married, this house didn't seem to want any children. While other couples our age were beginning their families, we stood by the sidelines and bravely waved a victory flag for them, while time went flying by and we still were waiting.

At last we were expecting, but it ended in the loss of a little boy at the end of the first trimester. The second baby had anencephaly, a fatal neural tube disorder. That little girl also went on to Heaven before us.

The next step after that was genetic testing at Tulane Hospital. The doctors and nurses there suggested that if there was another non-viable pregnancy, we could terminate it. And what is the procedure to determine if a pregnancy is not viable?

We found out that there is no fool-proof way to determine that. As with many things in life, we are not meant to usurp the place of God and take matters into our own hands. It is not our place to make decisions like that concerning life and death. Anyone who does is setting a horrible precedent for a greater decline into evil choices.

Then we had a beautiful little girl who grew into a lovely young lady and is now a mother, teacher, and director of teachers. We named her Naomi.

Two years after that, we had another fatal pregnancy. This time, the placenta became a tumor which destroyed the life of the baby----and would have threatened my life if it returned, for then it would have been malignant. This is known as a molar pregnancy.

I was highly displeased with my house at that point. This house certainly had a habit of making me have rare phenomena! And the irony was that in order to monitor the possibility of the return of that tumor, I had to take a blood sample pregnancy test EVERY MONTH at the hospital for a WHOLE YEAR.

If it was a new technician, and they congratulated me, I didn't bother to explain. I just said thank you. It was too redundant to keep explaining such a bizarre reason for that test.

At last, that was over. Then......NOTHING happened. For nine years.....

...Until there was this very tiny little baby who came far too early and hovered precariously between life and death at some points. We named him Isaac, and he is now pursuing his master's degree at college, with plans to teach history on the college level.

We never got an explanation about why this house expelled him so early, but his doctor said it was actually better for him to be out. This house had developed beta strep infection. I had never heard of this, (of course!) and it usually does not occur until much closer to the end of a pregnancy. That type of infection can do serious damage to a developing baby, so this house was no longer a safe place for a baby.

There was no use asking why that happened; as usual, there were no answers. But at least this house became a good dairy for as long as needed!

I have to admit that this house was not irksome during the "great change". (Menopause) In fact, I have to say the change has been a relief---no more Dr. Jekyll---Mr. Hyde mood swings! Things have calmed down a good bit, and there has been no reappearance of a Monster House. I am trying to take good care of it, so it will never desire to take revenge on me.

Still, I know it won't last forever.

But the good news is that I will be able to trade it in for a much better model---one that will no longer be subject to decay, disease, or a carnal nature to cause contention within myself.

That is not my own idea, either---it is the plan of the one who designed this house in the first place. He is the one who will execute this plan, and He has already made provision for this.

The best part is that it will be completely redesigned to look like His glorious body, and the inner nature will be just like His, too.   The Designer's name is Jesus.

And as I get to know our Designer even better, the more I am thrilled at the thought of becoming just as He is. His love for us is what we have all been longing for, even though we may not have realized it. He is designing a better place for us to live…a forever Home.

"If there is a natural body, there is also a spiritual body."
1 Corinthians 15:44

"For we know that if the earthly tent we live in is destroyed, we have a building from God, an eternal house in heaven, not built by human hands." 2 Corinthians 5:1

This is His promise.

TREASURED

He took my pain and made a pearl---
It glistens brightest in His light.
And He wears it on His heart----
For I am His.

And when my heart was broken
In the hands of cruel ways,
He took my tears and made a jewel---
Just for Him.

He set it on His crown of gold
And all of Heaven smiles to see---
This jewel is my life redeemed---
Made for Him.

He enclosed me with His healing Love
Until a treasure formed within----
This pearl I prize so dearly now, I will not throw to pigs----
For I am His.

"The LORD their God will save his people on that day
as a shepherd saves his flock. They will sparkle in his land
like jewels in a crown." Zechariah 9:16

FINDING LOVE

My mother died when I was nine years old. It happened suddenly without any warning, like a massive dark storm appearing out of nowhere on a sunny day. She died from a horrible car wreck while we were on the way to my grandmother's house. On the inside I was screaming to the heavens, "Come back, Momma!" while on the outside I was running and playing with my cousins. At night I would dream she was back in the kitchen baking cookies as she used to do. In my dream, I walked into the kitchen and said, "I thought you were dead." And she answered, "It wasn't true." I didn't want it to be true, but it was. There was no going back to the way it used to be; she was not coming back. I would wake up, and she was not there.

I would have flash-backs, of something huge and dark filling up my horizon swiftly until it blocked everything out of sight--- this was the oncoming car that hit us. Then there was nothing but blackness; this is because I was in a coma for three days. When I came out of the coma, I found out that everything in my life had changed. I went into "survival mode"—shutting down memory, tears, and anything else that would hurt too much.

My father loved me, but he had so much pain from grief that he couldn't heal me. I grew up lost; I had no reason for existence other than satisfying me---and "me" couldn't be satisfied. At age 17, I was a stormy, moody girl who was severely depressed and starved for love. Then one day I found love; I had an encounter with Jesus. I was all alone at the time, at my family home, and He revealed Himself to me. I didn't physically see Him or audibly hear His voice, but He came. He came because I called out to Him---and it was not in faith, either. It was in desperation. I had caught a glimpse of my real problem; and it was sin. I discovered I had a sin nature and it was self-destructive; it was killing me. I realized that day that this sin nature was opposite of the Lord's lovingkindness---and I could not love with a heart like this. I gave myself up to the Lord that day----and He took me in and loved me.

After that, it felt like I had a fairy tale life, although the daily struggles of overcoming things were very real. I went to college and finished in art, then I was married to the guy I had admired for five years who never noticed me until then! We worked in children's ministry and we were so happy and fulfilled in it, that twenty-one years went by in the blink of an eye.

Then I went through another death---the death of ministry. It happened suddenly, without warning, like a collision---and then we spent a long time picking up the pieces. I was all alone again, and Jesus came to me and spoke so tenderly to me, that I fell in love with Him all over again. Some may have wondered why we didn't move on; why did we stay? The answer is really simple; Jesus didn't allow it. He basically said, "This is your family." He wanted us to stay and reveal by our lives that He is our victory---over many kinds of death. His anointing can birth new life in us; intimacy with Him can create new gifts and abilities we didn't know were there. While all alone, I had to learn to REALLY believe in His love for me, in a way I didn't before when I was part of the "hub" of things.

I found out He truly comes close to those who have a broken heart. He does not despise a broken heart; His love intensifies for the one who is hurting, because He is the most compassionate Person in the universe. He gives us this compassion to share with others, too. This is His character; He laid down His life for us and shed His blood for us.

I discovered in a deeper way how much Jesus desires intimacy with me. My worship has become a hundred times more passionate because this is how I express my love to Him, and He enjoys it. "Nothing can separate us from His love" has a far greater meaning to me now.

Staying sweet in a bitter world is only possible through having intimate times with Jesus. Even our Christian church "culture" can condition us in ways that camouflage the love and passion of Jesus for His bride. We become "churchified" and we're working for the esteem of our church instead of treating Jesus as our Lover and our Husband. One day I was reading in Hosea 2, and I realized this is what Jesus had done for me: (This is from the NLT version)

> "I will lead her into the desert
> and speak tenderly to her there.
> I will return her vineyards to her
> and transform the Valley of Trouble
> into a gateway of hope.
> She will give herself to me there,
> as she did long ago when she was young,
> when I freed her from her captivity in Egypt.
> When that day comes," says the LORD,
> "you will call me 'my husband'
> instead of 'my master.'"

The NASB version says, "She will sing there as in the days of her youth." Hosea 2:15 These days, the thing I enjoy most is singing to Him. And He calls me His songbird.

THE COVENANT

I belong to you, o Lord.

There is no greater joy than this.

You bought me;

You paid the price with blood.

This cup and this bread are my contract;

I realize that I have entered

Into a covenant with You.

Stamp your image on my face;

Mark me as Your own.

Keep me forever

In the Holy of Holies

In the presence of Your Spirit,

In the way of life.

"This cup is the new covenant in my blood; do this,
whenever you drink it, in remembrance of me."

1 Corinthians 11:25

SONGS

This next section of writing is a collection of song lyrics.

Though I am certainly not an accomplished musician,
the Lord began giving me songs years ago,
and recently He gave some new songs to me.

I am not a skilled song writer; these songs come to me in
much the same way as a prophecy does.

He gives me the words, the melody, and a simple piano
accompaniment for the song.

You will see that the Lord is speaking directly
to us in some of these songs.

CAPTAIN OF OUR SALVATION

When the storms of life beset you---

And you don't know where to turn---

It would seem that you're about to go under---

And the waves, they keep coming strong----

There is One whose hand is reaching out;

Take His hand and He'll save you---

He's the Captain of our salvation and the guide for our ship;

Trust Him, let Him steer, and you won't have to fear---

He's the Captain of our salvation and the guide for our ship.

Oh, believe in Him, believe in Him, believe in Him

He will show you great and mighty things

That you do not know---

Oh believe in Him, believe in Him, believe in Him

When the waters get rough…when the waters get rough.

He has given us power over Satan

And we don't have to drown anymore—

If you'll take His hand, He will save you—

And deliver you from the storm.

And His name, His name is Jesus

Take His hand and He'll save you---

He's the Captain of our salvation

And the guide for our ship

Trust Him, let Him steer, and you won't have to fear

Oh, believe in Him, believe in Him, believe in Him

He will show you great and mighty things

That you do not know---

Oh believe in Him, believe in Him, believe in Him

When the waters get rough...when the waters get rough.

"Call to me and I will answer you and tell you great and
unsearchable things you do not know."

Jeremiah 33:3

"He stilled the storm to a whisper;
the waves of the sea were hushed."

Psalm 107:29

I'M LOOKING FOR A PEOPLE

I'm looking for a people who want to be set free

I'm looking for a people who want to worship me

In Spirit and in truth

Don't let any man spoil you with his philosophy;

Don't let any man take away your liberty;

Take my yoke and learn of me

I am meek and lowly

And you will find rest for your soul, for your soul.

I'm looking for a people who will seek my face

I'm looking for a people who will live by grace

To love me and one another

Don't let any man steal away your unity

I died to make you one to live in harmony

Take my yoke and learn of me

For my burden is light

And you will find rest for your soul, for your soul.

He is holy, He is love

He is holy, He is love

I BELONG TO HIM

Once upon a time, many years ago,

A young girl stood crying, not knowing where to go.

She was looking for love, she was looking for life.

And the only home she'd ever known was filled up with strife.

Then from somewhere she heard His voice—

Calling out her name.

Give your life to Me, child—you will never be the same.

I'm your strength when you are weak;

I'm the treasure that you seek—

And you'll be happy to belong to Me.

Suddenly she saw herself, and the problem within;

How could she ever love with a heart full of sin?

So she gave her life away to the One who set her free.

I know this story's true 'cause that girl was me.

Oh there in that tiny room He forgave all my sin.

Someday I'm going to live with Him.

He's my strength when I am weak;

He's the treasure that I seek.

And I'm so happy I belong to Him.

Now I have His Word to guide me all through the day.

When trouble comes, I know He hears me when I pray.

Oh, there in that tiny room, He forgave all my sin.

Someday I'm going to live with Him.

He's my strength when I am weak;

He's the treasure that I seek.

And I'm so happy I belong to Him....

and you'll be happy....

To belong to Him.

"Now this is what the LORD says.
He created you, people of Jacob;
he formed you, people of Israel.
He says, "Don't be afraid, because I have saved you.
I have called you by name, and you are mine."

Isaiah 43:1 NCV

"you do not belong to the world,
but I have chosen you out of the world."

John 15:19

KEEP THAT LOVE OF JESUS

You've got that love of Jesus down in your soul,

You've got that love of Jesus down in your soul.

Remember when we met Him—

How the blessings surely flowed

The Word of God became your light, to show you what to do

No more searching, we know where we belong—

In the family of God.

You wrote our names in Your book of life,

We're adopted by You,

We are loved through and through

The Holy Spirit filled us, we were praising God in tongues,

 Worshiping our Lord.

Then you had to leave us, and I didn't know how you'd do

And I prayed to God that He would keep you,

Always keep you true

Then one day you came back, and our hearts rejoiced to see

That you still had that love of Jesus down in your soul

You still had that love of Jesus down in your soul

And if we all stay true to Him,

He's gonna bring us home again.

So if you have to leave us, just let us know how you do

And we'll pray to God that He will keep you,

Always keep you true

Then one day you'll come back

And our hearts will rejoice to see

That you still have that love of Jesus down in your soul

You still have that love of Jesus down in your soul

And if we all stay true to Him,

He's gonna bring us home again

Just keep that love of Jesus, keep that love of Jesus,

Keep that love of Jesus

Down in your soul. Oh, yeah......

This song was meant specifically for the friends I met through Chi Alpha Christian Fellowship, an organization on campus for college students. We had such sweet worship times together at college retreats, and daily prayer together kept us encouraged while at a secular university.

I knew that when we were finished at college, we might lose contact with one another and that made me sad.

I look forward to that day when believers will be reunited together in the Lord's forever Kingdom.

ETERNAL LOVE

Through all the years of your life

And where ever your path may lead;

His love for you will go on and on;

His love for you will go on and on.

If you call out His name, He will answer you;

If you're lost and afraid, He will rescue you;

Don't walk away, don't walk away

Don't walk away from His love, His love.

Though darkness comes and you can't see at all

Hold His hand and you won't fall

He said, I will uphold you with My right hand

I will uphold you with My right hand.

Though the path is steep, I will steady you.

When you cannot walk, I will carry you.

Don't let go, don't let go

Don't let go of My hand, My hand.

I gave my body, I bled and died

To always have you at my side.

I faced your darkest fear of all

When they laid my body in the grave

But my love was stronger than death could ever be

Nothing can keep me from you.

Think of a thousand years from now

I will still be, still be loving you.

All I have promised will all come true

I will never, never leave you.

For My love for you is eternal love;

I have given you My word.

I have given you My word.

I have given you My word.

"Since these children are people with physical bodies, Jesus himself became like them. He did this so that, by dying, he could destroy the one who has the power of death—the devil— and free those who were like slaves all their lives because of their fear of death."

Hebrews 2:14-15 NCV

ON WINGS OF GRACE

Long ago you saw me

When I was formed in secret;

And you knew me, and you loved me.

All my days were written in your book of heaven;

Not one of them will ever be forgotten.

Through the darkest times, you were right by my side.

Even as a child, you were my unseen guide.

One day the time will come to leave this earth.

I know you will be there as you were at my birth;

Every day I live, help me dedicate to You.

Help me pray with child-like faith, when my life is through.

Now I lay me down to sleep

I pray the Lord my soul to keep

And I will be satisfied when I awake with your likeness

I know I will see your face

I'll soar with you on wings of grace

Wings of grace, wings of grace.

THE WISE MEN

Where is the one who's been born King of the Jews?
We have seen His star in the east
And we have pledged our lives to find this Child
We have come to worship Him.
Though it cost us everything to find this child
Though it might take years of our lives, we won't turn aside
Still our hearts are fixed on this one thing:
We've got to find Him, we've got to find Him.
Do you know the one who's been born King of the Jews?
For we have seen His star in the east
We do not seek for alms of healing or grace
We only want to see His face
We thought that such a holy child would be treated as a king
But on the night that He was born He was left out in the cold
Still we know this child must be the one the prophets
foretold.
How would we find Him? We've got to find Him.

The star that we'd seen in the sky from afar
Came and stood o'er the place where the baby lay
All our plans and dreams were fulfilled that night
As we knelt and worshipped Him.
We knew that this tiny child was the one sent by God

His name would be the only hope this world will ever know;

How our hearts rejoiced as we went on our way

We have found Him, I know we found Him.

Savior of the world, our eyes have seen Him

King who lives forever, I know we found Him

Ooooh, we found Him, I know we found Him

"In his name the nations will put their hope."

Matthew 12:21

After Jesus was born in Bethlehem
in Judea, during the time of King Herod,
Magi from the east came to Jerusalem and asked,

"Where is the one who has been born king of the Jews? We
saw his star when it rose and have come to worship him."

Matthew 2:1-2

"One who loves a pure heart and who speaks
with grace will have the king for a friend."

Proverbs 22:11

NEVER LAND

There's a land that I have heard of----

Where there will never be a night;

There's a king who lives forever, and His glory is our light.

With his blood He bought my pardon,

Though sin had captured me;

With His life He paid my ransom,

And his grace has set me free.

There will never be a need there;

He will wipe away our tears;

You will never come to harm there,

He will take away our fears.

There will never be a death there,

For our lives will never end;

We will never face rejection, for the King will be our friend.

In the Kingdom of Light--- there will never be a night

And the glory of His love will be like sunshine on our face

We will dwell forever in His amazing grace

His kingdom never ends; His mercy never ends.

There's a time that I've heard of, when He's coming for me

It's the time that I've longed for,

When at last my soul will be free.

Then at last I will see Him....face to face...

I'll see the One who gave me purity,

And took away my disgrace.

Give your life to Him, He will take you by the hand

With open arms He will welcome you into His land

In His book of life, He will write down your name

You will be His citizen, there will be no shame

In the Kingdom of light--- there will never be a night

And the glory of His love will be like sunshine on our face

We will dwell forever in His amazing grace

His kingdom never ends; His mercy never ends.

Now is the time to surrender your heart
to the King of all kings....to the King of all Kings....
He waits for you....He waits for you.

"He will wipe every tear from their eyes.
There will be no more death or mourning or crying or pain,
for the old order of things has passed away."
Revelation 21:4

HOPE THAT NEVER DIES

Traveling down a long, dusty dark road

Weary and cold, we wondered what would the future hold?

Then we saw who walked beside us—

A woman great with child.

And we wondered who she was; she had hope in her eyes.

Later on we heard the news of the child born that night.

Shepherds told of angels singing in great light;

They told them that the child was born

To save the human race.

And we trembled when we looked into the baby's face...

We have found the hope that never dies;

Now we have seen Him with our eyes—

He's alive---Messiah. He's alive---Messiah.

And every broken dream, every shattered hope,

Every ruined faith

Can be reborn in His light.

Two thousand years have passed

Since that night in Bethlehem.

We know the promise still remains that He will come again.

But he did not leave us orphans, He gave us a guide.

He sent the Holy Spirit to live inside;

He gave us the Word of God to know this story's true;

How the Father sent His only son to rescue me and you.

His body was the sacrifice to save the human race

And one day soon we'll see His love face to face.

We have found the hope that never dies;

Though you cannot see Him with your eyes,

He's alive----He rose again. He's alive---He rose again.

And every broken dream, every shattered hope,

Every ruined faith

Can be reborn in His light; can be reborn in His light.

So come Lord Jesus.....come.

Your birth, Lord, was the beginning of the end----
the end of sorrow and grief, the end of pain and suffering,
the end of guilt and shame, the end of Death.

His promises are eternal; they will never end.
He came once as a baby;
He will come back as our eternal King.

"We are receiving a kingdom which cannot be shaken."

Hebrews 12:28

LORD YOU SEE ME

Lord you see me from Your throne in Heaven

And you hear my cry---from Your throne on high

And you answer me.

You comfort me with Your holy words

In You I find all I need

You are all I need.

Lord you are my fortress, my place of refuge

And you shelter me, in Your arms of love

You rescue me.

You guard my heart with unfailing love

And you give to me your peace.

And you give me your peace.

I am yours forever, I am yours forever

There is no one else like You.

There is no one else like You.

ONE THING THE DEVIL FORGOT

The devil came along and he knocked me down

He said you'll never get up again.

But there's one thing that the devil forgot---

He forgot who is holding my hand.

The Lord pulled me up---out of the sinking sand.

The Lord pulled me up! And I know who is holding my hand.

The devil came along and he said you're a fool

And you'll never do anything right.

But there's one thing that the devil forgot----

He forgot who is in this fight.

The Lord fights for me! I can't do this on my own.

The Lord fights for me! And I know I'm never alone.

The devil came along and he said you're weak

And your life is filled with shame.

But there's one thing that the devil forgot---

He forgot who knows my name.

The Lord chooses me! I will never be the same.

The Lord chooses me! He called me by my name.

I will live my life always to praise Him.

The way He loves me always will amaze me.

The devil came along and he said it's dark

And you never will find your way.

But there's one thing that the devil forgot---

He forgot that it's almost day.

The Lord is my light! And His Word shows me the way

The Lord is my light! And He guides me in His way.

All the way home, all the way home.....to Him.

"The night is nearly over; the day is almost here.
So let us put aside the deeds of darkness
and put on the armor of light."

Romans 13:12

"Do not gloat over me, my enemy!
Though I have fallen, I will rise.
Though I sit in darkness,
the LORD will be my light."

Micah 7:8

HE WILL COME

He will come with clouds descending

We will rise to meet Him in the air

Our Savior, Friend, our true love will meet us there

He's preparing a banquet

For the redeemed of the Lord.

He invites all to come

All who are willing may come

To the marriage supper of the Lamb

Who was slain for our sin

Every tribe and nation will be there

Rejoicing in His holy love

Standing in a multitude around the throne of God

We will cast all our crowns at the feet of Jesus

For He alone is worthy of our praise.

The scars on His hands and feet

Are the marks of His love.

We will await that day---oh that glorious day!

On that day, the travail of His soul

Will be satisfied, so satisfied

Within the gates of Heaven

Are the people He desired

To live with Him, to belong to Him---

For eternity, for eternity…

He will come with clouds descending

We will rise to meet Him in the air,

Our Savior, Friend, our true love

Will meet us there---

So we will ever be with the Lord.

"For the Lord himself will come down from heaven, with a loud command, with the voice of the archangel and with the trumpet call of God, and the dead in Christ will rise first. After that, we who are still alive and are left will be caught up together with them in the clouds to meet the Lord in the air. And so we will be with the Lord forever."

1 Thessalonians 4:16-17

DOOR TO HEAVEN

Darkness hung over the earth like a cloud----

The man kneeling cried

He said, "Father if you will, take this cup from me

Yet not as I will but yours be done

Forever and ever Your will be done.

Long before the light of the sun broke through the night---

The man kneeling rose

He said, "Satan is coming, but he has nothing in me—

I go to my death willingly.

I love you forever, I always will.

In my Father's house are many rooms for you

I go to prepare a place for you;

I want my home to be your home too

I want you to see my glory.

When all is ready, I will come back for you

This is my joy, my joy----

When the morning sun turned to afternoon light---

The man on the cross died.

He cried, Father forgive them,

For they know not what they do

I shed my blood to rescue you

I am the door to Heaven, I open for you, for you…

Why spend your life on worthless things

Never knowing the joy that my love brings?

I am all you long for, all you ever dream

My gifts are waiting for you---for you….

I am all you long for, all you ever dream

My door is open---come fellowship with Me

For eternity, for eternity----my door is open,

Come in….

"Father, I want those you have given me to be with me where I am, and to see my glory, the glory you have given me because you loved me before the creation of the world."

John 17:24

"Ask and it will be given to you; seek and you will find; knock and the door will be opened to you."

Matthew 7:7

HE TOOK MY HEART BY SURPRISE

My day began like any other; I went to the well to get water

Then I saw Him sitting by the well

And He asked me to give Him a drink.

Why do you ask me---you must not know me;

I'm the very last person you should ask.

He said, "Oh, yes I know you---

You're the very person I want to ask.

I want to give you living water if only you would ask."

Sir, I said, you must be mistaken.

Are you greater than my forefather Jacob?

For he gave us this well

And besides you have nothing to draw water.

He said "All who drink from this well you see

Will always thirst again

But all who drink my living water will never thirst again."

Sir, I said, give me this water---

I'm so tired of always coming to this well

He said "Go and find your husband

And bring him to the well."

I said, Sir, I have no husband

And He said "I know this is true

And I know all your troubles, and I see all you do."

Sir, I said, I see you are a prophet

And I know you'll say my worship is all wrong

But I know when Messiah comes he'll help us

He will tell us all we need to know;

Then He said "I who speak to you am He

For the time has now come

And all who drink my living water

Will worship in Spirit and in truth;

Lay your burdens down

Lay your burdens down

I will set you free

Just drink of Me just drink of Me

Just drink of Me just drink of Me"

He took my heart by surprise

And now I know His living water

Lay your burdens down

Lay your burdens down

He will set you free

Just drink of Him just drink of Him

Just drink of Him just drink of Him

He took my heart by surprise

And now I know His living water

Don't you want some living water?

Don't you want some living water?

Don't you want some living water?

He'll give you living water.

Living water

YOU HAVE SHOWN ME LIFE

There I stood by the well, in a desert land.

No one to talk to or hold my hand

I did not choose this! Oh, God, if you are there

Hear my cry, hear my cry

Or I and the baby will die! I and the baby will die.

Suddenly an angel stood there beside me

And he called me by my name

Hagar, where have you come from?

Hagar, where are you going?

I'm running away from my home and my mistress

No one to care for me, no one to miss us

I did not choose this! Oh, God, if you care

Hear my cry, hear my cry

Or all my hope will die! All my hope will die.

Suddenly I saw in the angel's eyes, compassion for me.

Hagar, the Lord sees your pain

Hagar, the Lord knows your misery.

You must return to your home and your mistress

But I will care for you, I will watch over you.

You did not choose this, but I will bless you

You and the child will not die, you and the child will not die.

Then the angel left me, but I knew that
God had heard my cry, He heard my cry
I named that well the One who sees
You are the God who hears my cry
You are the God who sees me
You are the God who knows me

I named the child Ishmael as the angel said
Someone to talk to, to hold my hand
I did not choose this, but still You blessed me
I and the child did not die, I and the child did not die.
You have shown me life! You have shown me life.
You have shown me life! You have shown me life.

The story of Hagar and her child Ishmael
can be found in Genesis chapters 16, 17, and 21.

Sometimes things happen to us that are out of our control,
and we find ourselves in predicaments that we did not
choose. Other people exerted their will on our lives, and
made choices that brought us pain. Even in the midst of
this, the Lord can bless us in our situations. He does not
always right the wrong, but He brings great good out of it.
The greatest blessing is that He reveals Himself to us, and
His presence is with us as our greatest comfort.

ABOUT THE AUTHOR

Teresa Lavergne was involved in children's ministry for over thirty years. She was part of a church staff for twenty-one of those years, working with her husband in children's ministry. Together, they created theater productions for children which presented the Gospel message in creative, dramatic, and imaginative ways. They have published some of their skits and plays for ministry, and hope to publish more. In the last five years, Teresa has been writing devotionals and has published two children's Christian fiction fantasy books.

www.ingramcontent.com/pod-product-compliance
Lightning Source LLC
Chambersburg PA
CBHW061826040426
42447CB00012B/2833